Paul Kalanithi

Biography

Before Breath Fades Away

TABLE OF CONTENTS

PROLOGUE

PROLOGUE

Webster was much possessed by death
And saw the skull beneath the skin;
And breastless creatures underground
Leaned backward with a lipless grin.

—T. S. Eliot, "Whispers of Immortality"

As I flipped through the CT scan pictures, the diagnosis became clear. A whole liver lobe was obliterated, the spine was malformed, and the lungs were covered in countless tumors. cancer that spreads widely. I was starting my last year of training as a neurosurgical resident. In the unlikely event that a procedure would help the patient, I had reviewed scores of these scans over the previous six years. This scan, however, was unique because it was mine.

I wasn't in my white coat and scrubs in the radiology suite. The nurse had left a computer in my hospital room, and I was using it while wearing a patient's gown, attached to an IV pole, and accompanied by my internist wife, Lucy. In the hopes of discovering something that would alter the diagnosis, I repeated each sequence: the lung window, the bone window, the liver window, scrolling from top to bottom, then left to right, then front to back, as I had been taught to do.

On the hospital bed, we lay together.

"Do you think there's any possibility that it's something else?" Lucy asked softly, as though reading from a script.

"No," I replied.

Like young lovers, we clung to one another. We both suspected that I had a cancer growing inside of me during the past year, but we wouldn't accept it or even talk about it.

I had begun losing weight and experiencing excruciating back pain about six months prior. My belt tightened by one and then two notches when I got dressed in the morning. I visited my primary care physician, a former Stanford classmate. She had taken a maternal watch on my health because her sister had passed away unexpectedly while interning in neurosurgery after getting a virulent infection. But when I arrived, I discovered my classmate was on maternity leave, so there was another doctor in her office.

On a cold examination table, wearing a thin blue gown, I explained the symptoms to her. "Obviously," I replied, "if this were a question on a board exam—a 35-year-old with recently developed back pain and unexplained weight loss—the obvious response would be (C) cancer. Maybe I'm just working too hard. I'm not sure. To be sure, I would like to have an MRI.

She suggested getting X-rays first. The cost of MRIs for back pain is high, and unnecessary imaging has recently emerged as a key national focus area for cost reduction. However, the value of a scan also depends on your search criteria: For cancer, X-rays are essentially useless. However, many doctors consider ordering an MRI at this early stage of apostasy. "It makes sense to start there, even though X-rays aren't perfectly sensitive," she added.

"How about flexion-extension X-rays? Perhaps isthmic spondylolisthesis is a more accurate diagnosis in this case."

I could see her searching for it on Google from the reflection in the wall mirror.

"Up to 5% of people have a pars fracture, which is a common cause of back pain in young people."

"All right, I'll place the order."

"Thank you," I replied.

Why did I appear so meek in a patient's gown but so powerful in a surgeon's coat? In actuality, I was more knowledgeable about back pain than she was because I had studied spine disorders for half of my neurosurgeon training. Perhaps, though, a spondy was more likely. A sizable percentage of young adults were impacted—and you had spine cancer in your thirties? It is impossible for the odds to be greater than one in ten thousand. It would still be less common than a spondy even if it were 100 times more common than that. Perhaps I was simply making myself anxious.

The X-rays appeared to be normal. We attributed the symptoms to aging and hard work, made an appointment for a follow-up, and I returned to complete my final case of the day. Back pain subsided and weight loss slowed. There weren't many of these exhausting, fourteen-hour days left, so I got through the day with a good dose of ibuprofen. After ten years of unrelenting training, I was nearly finished with my journey from medical student to neurosurgery professor. I was resolved to keep going for the next fifteen months, until my residency was over. I was receiving job offers from several major universities, had won prestigious national awards, and had gained the respect of my seniors. Recently, my Stanford program director sat me down and told me, "Paul, I believe you'll be the top applicant for any position you apply for." Just so you know, we'll be hiring faculty to find someone just like you. Of course, there are no guarantees, but it's something to think about.

When I arrived at the summit of the mountain at the age of thirty-six, I was able to see the Promised Land, which included the Mediterranean Sea, Jericho, and Gilead. On that sea, I could spot a nice catamaran that Lucy, our imaginary kids, and I would use on the weekends. As my work schedule relaxed and my life became easier to handle, I could feel the tension in my back releasing. I could envision myself at last fulfilling my promise to be a husband.
A few weeks later, I started experiencing intense chest pains. Had I run into something on the job? Somehow cracked a rib? I would occasionally wake up on sweat-soaked sheets. I started losing weight again, faster this time, going from 175 to 145 pounds. I started to cough a lot. There was little question. Lucy and I were waiting to meet her sister in San Francisco's Dolores Park on a Saturday afternoon while we lay in the sun. She took a quick look at my phone's screen,

which showed the results of a search in a medical database: "frequency of cancers in thirty- to forty-year-olds."

"What?" she said. "I didn't realize you were actually worried about this."
I didn't respond. I didn't know what to say.
"Do you want to tell me about it?" she asked.
She was upset because she had been worried about it, too. She was upset because I wasn't talking to her about it. She was upset because I'd promised her one life, and given her another.
"Can you please tell me why you aren't confiding in me?" she asked.
I turned off my phone. "Let's get some ice cream," I said.

———

The following week, we were going to New York for a vacation to see some old college pals. Perhaps a few cocktails and a restful night's sleep would help us rekindle our relationship and relieve some of the strain on our marriage.
Lucy, however, had another idea. A few days before the trip, she declared, "I'm not coming to New York with you." She wanted time to think about the status of our marriage, so she was planning to move out for a week. She spoke in even tones, which made me even dizzy.

"What?" "I said." "No."
"This is so confusing because I love you so much," she said. However, I'm concerned that our goals for our relationship are different. We seem to be halfway connected. I don't want to unintentionally find out about your concerns. You don't seem to find it problematic when I talk to you about feeling alone. I must take a different approach.
I assured them that everything would be alright. "It's only a residency."
Was it really that bad? Our marriage had undoubtedly suffered due to neurosurgical training, which is one of the most demanding and demanding medical specialties. There were numerous occasions when I arrived home from work late, after Lucy had gone to bed, and collapsed on the floor of the living room, exhausted, and numerous

occasions when I left for work early in the morning, before she had woken up. However, we were at the height of our careers at this point, and most universities wanted both of us—Lucy in internal medicine, me in neurosurgery. We had made it through the most challenging portion of our trip. Had we not talked about this a dozen times? She knew this was the worst time for her to blow things up, didn't she? Did she not realize that I loved her, that we were so close to living the life we had always dreamed of together, and that I only had one year left in residency?

"I could make it if it were just residency," she remarked. "We have come this far. But what if it's more than just residency? That's the issue. Do you genuinely believe that things will improve once you attend academic neurosurgery?

She insisted that she needed time—alone—but I offered to forego the trip, to be more forthcoming, to see the couples therapist Lucy had recommended a few months prior. Only a hard edge remained after the fuzziness of the confusion vanished. Alright, I replied. I would guess the relationship was over if she made the decision to leave. I wouldn't tell her if it turned out that I had cancer; she would be allowed to lead her own life.

I sneaked into a couple doctor's appointments to rule out some common cancers in young people before I left for New York. (Testicular? Melanoma, no? No, leukemia? No.) As usual, neurosurgery was very busy. I spent 36 hours straight in the operating room on a number of extremely complicated cases, including giant aneurysms, intracerebral arterial bypasses, and arteriovenous malformations, so Thursday night turned into Friday morning. When the attending arrived, I silently thanked them and took a few minutes to lean my back against a wall. Only when I was leaving the hospital and traveling home before going to the airport was I able to get a chest X-ray. I reasoned that if I had cancer, this might be my last chance to see my friends, or if I didn't, there was no reason to call off the trip.

I hurried home to get my belongings. Lucy informed me that she had arranged for us to attend couples therapy as she drove me to the airport.

I texted her from the gate, saying, "I wish you were here."

After a few minutes, the reply was, "I love you." When you return, I'll be here.

During the flight, my back became extremely stiff. By the time I arrived at Grand Central to board a train to my friends' upstate location, I was in excruciating pain. I've experienced back spasms of various intensities over the past few months, ranging from minor discomfort that I could ignore to pain that caused me to stop talking and grind my teeth to pain so bad that I screamed while curled up on the ground. The intensity of this pain was on the higher end of the spectrum. To prevent tears, I lay down on a hard bench in the waiting area, feeling my back muscles tense, breathing to manage the pain (the ibuprofen wasn't affecting this), and identifying each muscle as it spasmed: piriformis, latissimus, rhomboid, erector spinae, etc.

A security officer came over. "You can't lie down here, sir."

With a gasp, I said, "I apologize." "Back spasms"

"You're still not allowed to lie down here."

Sorry, cancer is killing me.

I kept saying the words, but what if I wasn't? Perhaps this is the reality of life for those with back pain. I was well-versed in the anatomy, physiology, and terminology used by patients to characterize various types of back pain, but I had no idea how it felt. Maybe that was all. Perhaps. Or perhaps the jinx wasn't something I wanted. It's possible that I simply didn't want to mention cancer aloud.

I got up and limped to the platform.

When I arrived at the house in Cold Spring, which is located on the Hudson River fifty miles north of Manhattan, it was late in the afternoon. A dozen of my best friends from previous years were there to greet me, and their cheers were drowned out by the sounds of contented young children. An icy dark and stormy made its way to my hand as hugs followed.

"No Lucy?"
"Sudden work thing," I said. "Very last-minute."
"Oh, what a bummer!"
"Say, do you mind if I put my bags down and rest a bit?"
I had hoped that a few days away from the operating room, along with enough rest, relaxation, and sleep—basically, a taste of normal life—would help my back pain and fatigue symptoms return to normal. However, it became evident after a day or two that there would be no relief.
I crept to the lunch table to gaze at the many plates of crab legs and cassoulet that I couldn't bring myself to eat, and I slept through breakfasts. I was worn out by dinner and ready to go back to sleep. The children mostly played on and around me, jumping and screaming, but occasionally I read to them. "I think Uncle Paul needs a break, kids. Would you mind playing over there? Fifteen years ago, I recalled a day off from summer camp counseling where I was sitting on the shore of a lake in Northern California, reading a book called Death and Philosophy, while a group of happy kids used me as an obstacle in a complicated game of Capture the Flag. The incongruities of that scene used to make me laugh: a twenty-year-old with his nose buried in a small black book about death, surrounded by the beauty of trees, a lake, mountains, and the chirping of birds mixed with the squeal of contented four-year-olds. Only now, at this precise moment, did I realize the similarities: the Hudson River replaced Lake Tahoe; the children were my friends rather than strangers; and my own body, dying, stood in for a book on death that separated me from the world around me.

I informed our host, Mike, on the third night that I would be ending the trip early and returning home the following day.
He remarked, "You don't look so great." "Is everything alright?"

"How about we take a seat and get some scotch?" "I said."

I said, "Mike, I think I have cancer," in front of his fireplace. Additionally, it is not the good kind.

I had never said it before.

"All right," he said. "I assume this isn't some kind of complex practical joke?"

"No."

He hesitated. "I'm not sure what to ask exactly."

"Well, I guess I should state up front that I am not positive that I have cancer. Since many of the symptoms suggest it, I'm just fairly certain of it. Tomorrow, I will return home and resolve the matter. I hope I'm mistaken.

To save me from having to carry my bags with me, Mike offered to take them and mail them home. The following morning, he took me to the airport, and I arrived in San Francisco six hours later. As soon as I got off the plane, my phone rang. My primary care physician called with the results of a chest X-ray; my lungs appeared blurry rather than clear, as if the camera's aperture had been left open for too long. According to the doctor, she had no idea what that meant.

She probably understood what it meant.

I was aware.

I didn't tell Lucy until we got home, even though she picked me up from the airport. She knew when I told her while we were sitting on the couch. The distance between us disappeared as she rested her head on my shoulder.

I said in a whisper, "I need you."

"I promise never to abandon you," she declared.

We requested that I be admitted by calling a close friend who works as a neurosurgeon at the hospital.

I put on the familiar light blue hospital gown, was given the plastic arm bracelet that all patients wear, passed the nurses I knew by name, and was shown to a room—the same room where I had seen hundreds of patients over the years. I had sat with patients in this room and explained complicated operations and terminal diagnoses; I had congratulated them on their recovery from a disease and witnessed their joy at being able to resume their lives; and I had declared patients dead. I had changed the calendar, scribbled instructions on the marker board, cleaned my hands in the sink, and sat in the chairs. At times when I was completely worn out, I had even wished I could just lie down in this bed and sleep. I lay there now, completely conscious.

I didn't recognize the young nurse who stuck her head in.

"The physician will arrive shortly."

The future I had envisioned, the one that was about to come to pass as the result of decades of hard work, vanished with that.

PART 1
In Perfect Health I Begin

The hand of the LORD was upon me, and carried me out in the spirit of the LORD, and set me down in the midst of the valley which was full of bones,
And caused me to pass by them roundabout: and, behold, there were very many in the open valley; and, lo, they were very dry.
And he said unto me, Son of man, can these bones live?
—Ezekiel 37:1–3, King James translation

I was positive I would never be a doctor. I relaxed on a desert plateau just above our house, stretching out in the sun. Earlier that day, my uncle—a doctor like so many of my relatives—asked me what I wanted to do for a living. Since I was leaving for college, the question hardly registered. I guess I would have replied "writer" if you had made me choose, but to be honest, the idea of any career at this stage seemed ridiculous. I felt more like a buzzing electron ready to reach escape velocity and launch myself into an unfamiliar and glittering universe than someone getting ready to climb a career ladder as I prepared to leave this small Arizona town in a few weeks.

The town of fifteen thousand, six hundred miles from my new college dorm at Stanford and all its promise, seemed to be getting smaller as I lay there in the dirt, surrounded by sunlight and memories.

Growing up, I only knew medicine by its absence—more precisely, the absence of a father who left for work before sunrise and came home in the dark to a plate of reheated dinner. My father moved us three boys, ages eight, ten, and fourteen, from Bronxville, New York, a small, wealthy suburb just north of Manhattan, to Kingman, Arizona, in a desert valley surrounded by two mountain ranges, when I was ten years old. The outside world knew Kingman, Arizona, mainly as a place to stop for gas on the way to somewhere else. The sun, the cost of living (how else would he afford to send his sons to the universities he wanted to attend), and the chance to start his own regional cardiology practice were what drew him in. He quickly gained respect from the community for his unwavering commitment to his patients. "It's very easy to be number one: find the guy who is number one, and score one point higher than he does," he said, combining stony pronouncements with hugs, kisses, and austere diktats with sweet affections when we did see him, which was usually late at night or on the weekends. In his mind, he had come to a compromise that fatherhood could be reduced to brief, intense, and sincere bursts of intensity that could be equivalent to whatever it was that other fathers did. I just knew that if that was the cost of the medication, it was just too much.

From my desert plateau, I could see our home at the foot of the Cerbat Mountains, just outside the city limits, surrounded by red-rock desert dotted with paddle-shaped cacti, tumbleweeds, and mesquite. Dust devils whirled up out here, obscuring your vision, and then vanished. Long stretches of space were followed by a descent into the distance. Max and Nip, our two dogs, never got bored with independence. They would go out every day and return home with some new desert treasure, such as a deer leg, leftover jackrabbit pieces to eat later, a horse's sun-bleached skull, or a coyote's jawbone.

My friends and I also enjoyed the freedom. We would spend our afternoons walking, exploring, and searching for rare desert creeks and bones. The wild, windy desert was strange and seductive to me because I had spent my previous years in a Northeastern suburb with a candy store and a main street lined with trees. When I was ten years old, I came upon an old irrigation grate on my first hike by myself. I used my fingers to pry it open, and when I raised it up, I saw three white silken webs a few inches from my face. Inside each, a glistening black bulbous body with the dreaded blood-red hourglass shining on it was marching along on spindled legs. With the impending birth of innumerable more black widows, a pale, pulsating sac breathed close to each spider. Horror closed the grate with a crash. I staggered back.

The combination of the inhuman posture, the black shine, the red hourglass, and the "country facts"—that nothing is more deadly than a black widow spider bite—were frightening. For years I suffered nightmares.

Tarantulas, wolf spiders, fiddlebacks, bark and whip scorpions, centipedes, diamondbacks, sidewinders, and Mojave greens were among the many terrifying creatures that could be found in the desert. We eventually became accustomed to these animals, even at ease with them. To have fun, my friends and I would drop an ant onto the outer edges of a wolf spider's nest and observe how its tangled escape attempts sent tremors down the silk strands into the spider's dark central hole. We would wait for the spider to finally burst from its hollows and grab the doomed ant in its mandibles. I came to refer to the urban legend's rural cousin as "country facts." Country facts, as I first learned them, gave desert creatures fairy abilities, so the Gila monster, for example, was just as real as the Gorgon. We discovered that some country facts, such as the existence of the jackalope, had been purposefully made up to confuse city people and entertain the locals only after we had lived in the desert for a while. On one occasion, I spent an hour persuading a group of Berlin exchange students that, indeed, there was a species of coyote that lived inside cacti and could jump ten yards to attack its prey—that is, unsuspecting Germans. However, in the midst of the swirling sand, nobody was exactly sure where the truth lay; for every absurd country fact, there was one that felt real and solid. For instance, it seemed common sense to always look for scorpions on your shoes.

I was expected to take my younger brother, Jeevan, to school when I was sixteen. As usual, I was late one morning. Jeevan was standing impatiently in the foyer, demanding that I hurry up because he didn't want to be detained again for being late. I hurried down the stairs and threw open the front door. and almost stepped on a six-foot rattlesnake that was sleeping. Another country fact was that, like Grendel's mother seeking retribution, a rattlesnake's mate and young would come and establish a permanent nest on your property if you killed it. Using a seriocomic dance, Jeevan and I were able to get the snake into the pillowcase after the unlucky person grabbed a pair of thick gardening gloves and a shovel and the lucky person grabbed a pillowcase. I then threw everything out into the desert like an Olympic hammer thrower, intending to get the pillowcase later that afternoon to avoid getting in trouble with our mother.

—

The main mystery of our early years was not why our father chose to move our family to the desert town of Kingman, Arizona, which we came to love, but rather how he persuaded my mother to accompany him there. From southern India to New York City, where she was a Hindu and he was a Christian, they had fled in love. Their marriage was condemned on both sides, and it caused years of family strife— my mother's mother insisted that I be called by my middle name, Sudhir, and never acknowledged my name, Paul—to Arizona, where my mother had to face an uncontrollable death phobia of snakes. She would lock the doors and arm herself with the closest large, sharp tool—rake, cleaver, or ax—after being frightened into the house by even the tiniest, cutest, and most harmless red racer.

Although the snakes were a continual source of worry, my mother was most concerned about the future of her children. My older brother, Suman, had almost finished high school in Westchester County, where prestigious universities were expected, prior to our move. Soon after arriving in Kingman, he was accepted to Stanford and soon after, he left home. We discovered, however, that Kingman was not Westchester. My mother was upset as she looked over the public school system in Mohave County. The U.S. census recently named Kingman America's least educated district. The percentage of high school dropouts was slightly over thirty percent. Few students continued their education, and none attended Harvard, my father's ideal university. My mother called friends and family from affluent

East Coast suburbs for advice, and while some were sympathetic, others were thrilled that their kids no longer had to compete with the Kalanithis, who had suddenly lost their access to education.

She started crying at night and sobbed by herself in her bed. My mother got a "college prep reading list" from somewhere because she was worried that the underfunded educational system would cripple her kids. She had not read many of the books on the list herself, having been trained as a physiologist in India, married at the age of 23, and busy with raising three children in a foreign land. However, she would ensure that her children were not deprived. When I was ten years old, she forced me to read 1984; while the sex scandalized me, it also made me appreciate language deeply.

As we methodically went through the list, we came across countless books and authors, including Dickens, Twain, Austen, Billy Budd, The Last of the Mohicans, Edgar Allan Poe, Robinson Crusoe, Ivanhoe, Gogol, and The Count of Monte Cristo. My brother Suman was sending me the books he had read in college, including The Prince, Don Quixote, Candide, Le Morte D'Arthur, Beowulf, Thoreau, Sartre, and Camus, when I was twelve years old. Some made a bigger impression than others. I argued that happiness was not the purpose of life in my college admissions essay, which was based on Brave New World, which also served as the foundation for my developing moral philosophy. I went through the typical teenage crises a thousand times with Hamlet. My friends and I had many happy misadventures during high school thanks to romantic poems like "To His Coy Mistress." We would frequently sneak out at night to perform songs like "American Pie" under the cheerleading captain's window. (We reasoned that since her father was a local minister, there was less chance of a shooting.) My anxious mother thoroughly questioned me about all the drugs that teenagers take after I was discovered returning at dawn from one of these late-night adventures. She had no idea that the volume of romantic poetry she had given me the week before had been the most intoxicating thing I had ever experienced. As finely honed lenses that offered fresh perspectives on the world, books turned into my closest confidants.

My mother drove us over a hundred miles north to Las Vegas, the closest large city, so we could take our PSATs, SATs, and ACTs as part of her efforts to ensure her kids received an education. She organized teachers, joined the school board, and pushed for the inclusion of AP courses in the curriculum. She was a phenomenon who decided to change the Kingman school system on her own initiative. At our high school, there was a sudden sense that the horizon was defined by what lay beyond the two mountain ranges that surrounded the town.

The school guidance counselor told my close friend Leo, who was the poorest kid I knew and our salutatorian, in his senior year, "You're smart—you should join the army."
He later told me about it. "Shit," he uttered. "I am also attending Harvard, Yale, or Stanford if you are."
I'm not sure which made me happier, Leo getting into Yale or me getting into Stanford.
Since Stanford started classes one month later than all the other schools, my friends dispersed, leaving me behind as the summer went on. I would often hike into the desert by myself in the afternoons to nap and reflect until my girlfriend, Abigail, left her job at Kingman's only coffee shop. Hiking was more enjoyable than driving, and the desert provided a shortcut through the mountains and down into town. Abigail was a Scripps College student in her early twenties who was taking a semester off to save money for tuition to avoid taking out loans. We would frequently meet after she got off work, and I was captivated by her worldliness and the feeling that she knew secrets that one could only learn in college because she had studied psychology. She was a sign of the new world that would be waiting for me in a few weeks, the sub rosa. When I woke up from a nap one afternoon, I noticed vultures circling, thinking I was carrion. It was nearly three

when I looked at my watch. I would have been late. After dusting off my jeans, I continued to jog through the desert until the sand turned to pavement, the first buildings emerged, and I turned the corner to see Abigail sweeping the coffee shop deck with a broom.

She said, "There won't be an iced latte for you today because I already cleaned the espresso machine."

We entered after the floors had been swept. Abigail picked up a paperback she had hidden there as she made her way to the cash register. She threw it at me and said, "Here." You ought to read this. Why don't you try something lowbrow for once? You're always reading such highbrow nonsense.

Jeremy Leven's book, Satan: His Psychotherapy and Cure by the Unfortunate Dr. Kassler, J.S.P.S., was five hundred pages long. I read it within a day after bringing it home. High culture wasn't present. It wasn't funny, although it should have been. But it did make the rash assumption that the mind was just the brain's function, which really got to me; it shocked my naïve perception of realities. It must be true, of course—otherwise, what were our brains doing? We were biological beings with free will, but the brain was an organ that was governed by all the laws of physics. The brain, then, was the apparatus that somehow made it possible for literature to give a rich account of human meaning. It appeared to be magic. I took out a highlighter and opened my red Stanford course catalog, which I had perused dozens of times, in my room that evening. I started looking into biology and neuroscience in addition to all the literature classes I had previously graded.

———

A few years later, I had almost finished degrees in human biology and English literature, but I hadn't given much more thought to a career. I was more motivated by a sincere desire to learn what makes human life meaningful than by a desire to succeed. I still believed that while neuroscience established the most elegant rules of the brain, literature offered the best description of the workings of the mind. Despite being a nebulous concept, meaning appeared to be inextricably linked to moral principles and interpersonal relationships. The Waste Land by T. S. Eliot struck a deep chord because it depicted loneliness, meaninglessness, and the desperate search for human connection. Eliot's metaphors began to seep into my own language. Other writers also discovered resonance. Nabokov, for his understanding of how our own pain can cause us to become indifferent to the apparent pain of another. Conrad, for his acute awareness of the profound impact misunderstandings can have on people's lives. Literature, in my opinion, offers the best resources for moral reflection besides shedding light on other people's experiences. I missed the messiness and gravity of actual human life, and my brief excursions into the formal ethics of analytical philosophy felt as dry as a bone.

My desire to create and fortify the human connections that constituted that meaning would clash with my monastic, academic study of human meaning throughout college. Was the unlived life worth examining if the unexamined life was not worth living? I applied for two jobs as I approached my sophomore summer: a prep chef position at Sierra Camp, a Stanford alumni family vacation destination on the immaculate shores of Fallen Leaf Lake, which borders the bleak beauty of Desolation Wilderness in Eldorado National Forest, and an internship at the highly scientific Yerkes Primate Research Center in Atlanta. Simply put, the camp literature promised the greatest summer of your life. Being accepted surprised and flattered me. However, I had recently discovered that macaques possessed a primitive culture, and I was excited to visit Yerkes to witness what might be the innate source of meaning. To put it another way, I could either experience meaning or study it.

I waited as long as I could before deciding to camp. I then went to my biology adviser's office to let him know what I had decided. As usual, he was seated at his desk with his head deep in a journal when I entered. He was a quiet, friendly man with heavy-lidded eyes, but when I told him about my plans, he changed completely. His eyes widened, his face flushed red, and there were spit droplets flying. "What?" he asked. "Are you going to be a chef or a scientist when you grow up?"

When the term finally ended, I was still a little concerned that my life had taken a wrong turn as I drove to camp up the windy mountain road. But my skepticism was fleeting. The camp fulfilled its promise by focusing on all the ideals of youth: richness in experience, friendships, and conversation; beauty in lakes, mountains, and people. It was possible to hike without a headlamp on full moon nights because the light filled the wilderness. With the clear, starry night reflected in the flat, still lakes spread out below, we would begin the trail at two in the morning and reach the closest peak, Mount Tallac, just before sunrise. With coffee someone had been considerate enough to bring, we survived icy gusts of wind while snuggled in sleeping bags at the summit, almost 10,000 feet above sea level. We would then sit and observe the stars gradually being erased as the first glimmer of sunlight, a faint shade of day blue, would peek out from the eastern horizon. Until the first ray of the sun appeared, the day sky would spread high and wide. The far-off roads of South Lake Tahoe came alive with the morning commuters. To the west, however, the night was still unconquered—pitch-black, stars in full gleam, the full moon still pinned in the sky—and if you cracked your head back, you could see the blue of the day darken halfway across the sky. The full light of day shone toward you to the east, while night ruled to the west without showing any signs of capitulation. This, between day and night, is the best way for any philosopher to describe the sublime. It seemed like God had just said, "Let there be light!" You could not help but feel like a speck in the vastness of the earth, the mountain, and the universe, but you could also feel your own feet on the talus, confirming your presence in the midst of the majesty.

Every day at Sierra Camp felt full of life and the relationships that give life purpose, even though it was summer and perhaps no different from any other camp. On other evenings, we gathered on the deck of the dining room to drink whiskey while talking about literature and the serious issues of post-adolescence with Mo, the camp's assistant director and a Stanford graduate on a break from his English PhD. In a summary of our time together, he sent me his first published short story after returning to his PhD the following year:

Suddenly, I know what I want. I want a pyre to be built by the counselors. I allowed my ashes to fall and mix with the sand. Lose my teeth in the sand, my bones in the driftwood. I don't think children or seniors have any wisdom. There comes a time, a threshold, when the minutiae of life wear down the accumulation of experience. Living in the present makes us wiser than ever.

—

I didn't miss the monkeys when I was back on campus. I continued to work for a deeper understanding of a life of the mind over the next two years because life felt full and rich. Through a variety of adventures, I deepened my relationships with a group of close friends, studied neuroscience and worked in an fMRI lab to learn how the brain could produce an organism capable of finding meaning in the world, and studied literature and philosophy to understand what makes life meaningful. We dressed as Mongols and raided the school cafeteria; we set up a whole phony fraternity in our co-op house, complete with phony rush-week activities; we posed in a gorilla suit in front of the gates at Buckingham Palace; we broke into Memorial Church at midnight to lie on our backs and listen to our voices echoing in the apse; and so on. (Then I found out that Virginia Woolf, after being properly reprimanded, stopped bragging about our insignificant antics after she once boarded a battleship disguised as Abyssinian royalty.)

In my senior year, we went to a home for individuals with severe brain injuries as part of one of my final neuroscience classes on ethics and neuroscience. A dejected wailing greeted us as we entered the main reception area. My eyes searched for the source of the noise while our guide, a gregarious woman in her 30s, introduced herself to the group. A large-screen television behind the reception desk was muted and playing a soap opera. As she begged someone off camera, a blue-eyed brunette with well-groomed hair and a slightly shaken head filled the screen. Zoom out and her strong-jawed, unmistakably gravel-voiced lover appeared; they gave each other a passionate embrace. The cries became louder. A young woman, perhaps twenty, with her hands balled into fists pressed into her eyes, rocking violently back and forth, wailing and wailing, was standing on a blue mat in front of the television. I approached to look at the counter. I saw glimpses of the back of her head as she rocked, a big, pale patch of skin where her hair had fallen out.

The group was departing to take a tour of the facility, so I moved aside to join them. I found out from the guide that many of the residents had almost drowned when they were young. I looked around and saw we were the only guests. Was that typical? I inquired.

A family will initially visit frequently, daily, or even twice a day, the guide explained. Then maybe every other day. Only weekends after that. After a few months or years, the visits gradually decrease until they only occur on special occasions like Christmas and birthdays. Most families eventually move as far as possible.

She said, "I don't blame them." "Taking care of these children is difficult."

I felt a raging rage. Tough? It was difficult, sure, but how could parents leave these children? In one room, the patients were laid out in neat rows like soldiers in a barracks, mostly motionless, on cots. I approached one of them and looked them in the eye. Her hair was tangled and dark, and she was in her late teens. I took a moment to try to show her that I cared by smiling. One of her hands was limp when I picked it up. However, she gurgled and grinned at me directly.

"I think she's smiling," I told the attendant.

"Could be," she said. "It can be hard to tell sometimes."

But I was sure of it. She was smiling.

When we got back to campus, I was the last one left in the room with the professor. "So, what'd you think?" he asked.

I vented openly about how I couldn't believe that parents had abandoned these poor kids, and how one of them had even smiled at me.

The professor was a mentor, someone who thought deeply about how science and morality intersected. I expected him to agree with me.

"Yeah," he said. "Good. Good for you. But sometimes, you know, I think it's better if they die."

I grabbed my bag and left.

She had been smiling, hadn't she?

Only later would I realize that our trip had added a new dimension to my understanding of the fact that brains cause our ability to form relationships and make life meaningful. Sometimes, they break.

—

I had a persistent feeling that I still had a lot of unanswered questions and that I wasn't finished studying as graduation approached. I was accepted into Stanford's master's program in English literature after applying. I now believe that language is a force that exists between people and brings our brains—which are protected by skulls that are only a centimeter thick—into communion. Only between people did a word have meaning, and the depth of the relationships we build determines the meaning and virtue of life. Meaning was based on the relational nature of people, or "human relationality." But in some way, this process was present in bodies and brains, susceptible to their own physiological demands and prone to malfunctioning. I reasoned that there must be some connection, however complicated, between the language of neurons, digestive tracts, and heartbeats and the language of life as experienced—of passion, hunger, and love.

I had the good fortune to study under Richard Rorty at Stanford, who was arguably the greatest living philosopher of his time. It was under his guidance that I started to see all fields of study as developing a vocabulary, a collection of instruments for gaining a specific understanding of human existence. Great literary works compelled the reader to use their own vocabulary by providing their own sets of tools. As part of my thesis, I read the writings of Walt Whitman, a poet who, a century earlier, was troubled by the same issues that plagued me and who sought to define and explain what he called "the Physiological-Spiritual Man."

As I completed my thesis, I could only draw the conclusion that Whitman had failed to develop a cohesive "physiological-spiritual" vocabulary, but at least his failures were instructive. Additionally, I was becoming more convinced that I didn't want to pursue literary studies any further because its primary concerns started to seem excessively political and anti-scientific. It would be hard for me to find a community in the literary world, according to one of my thesis advisers, because most English PhDs responded to science "like apes to fire, with sheer terror." I had no idea where my life was going. Despite being unconventional and incorporating as much history of psychiatry and neuroscience as literary criticism, my thesis, "Whitman and the Medicalization of Personality," was well received. In an English department, it didn't quite fit. In an English department, I didn't quite fit in.

I briefly contemplated joining my closest college friends who were moving to New York City to pursue careers in the arts, such as comedy, journalism, or television, and making a fresh start. However, I couldn't stop wondering: What connections existed between philosophy, literature, morality, and biology? One afternoon, with the autumn breeze blowing, I let my thoughts wander as I walked home from a football game. The voice I heard said, "Set aside the books and practice medicine," in contrast to Augustine's voice in the garden, which said, "Take up and read." Suddenly, it seemed clear. My father, my uncle, and my older brother were all doctors, but I had never considered medicine as a real possibility, maybe because of this.

Whitman himself, however, had claimed that "only the doctor could fully comprehend the Physiological-Spiritual Man".

I spoke with a pre med adviser the following day to work out the details. It would take roughly a year of rigorous coursework to prepare for medical school, plus an additional 18 months for the application process. It would entail leaving me behind so that my friends could continue to strengthen their bonds in New York. It would entail putting books aside. However, it would give me the opportunity to discover solutions that are not found in books, discover a new kind of sublime, develop empathy for the suffering, and continue to explore the question of what gives human life purpose despite death and decay.

I started taking as many chemistry and physics classes as I could to complete the required premedical coursework. I was reluctant to work part-time because I thought it would interfere with my studies, but since I couldn't afford the rent in Palo Alto, I climbed into an empty dorm room with an open window. I squatted for a few weeks before the caretaker, who was also a friend, found me. Along with some helpful warnings, such as when the high school girls' cheerleading camps would be arriving, she gave out a key to the room. I would pack a tent, some books, and some granola and go up to Tahoe until it was safe to return, reasoning that it would be prudent to avoid becoming a registered sex offender.

After my classes ended, I had a year off because the application process for medical school takes 18 months. Before I made the decision to permanently leave academia, a number of professors had advised me to get a degree in the history and philosophy of science and medicine. I applied to Cambridge's HPS program and was accepted. I spent the following year teaching in rural English classrooms, where I frequently made the case that developing strong moral opinions about life-or-death issues required firsthand experience. The words lost their weight and became as light as the breath that carried them. I took a step back and saw that all I was doing was reaffirming my instinct: I wanted that firsthand experience. I could only pursue a serious biological philosophy while working as a doctor. Compared to moral action, moral speculation was insignificant. After graduating, I returned to the United States. I was attending medical school at Yale.

—

You would think that cutting a dead person for the first time would make you feel a little amused. But oddly, everything seems normal. An air of propriety is created by the bright lights, stainless steel tables, and professors wearing bow ties. Nevertheless, that initial cut, which extends from the nape of the neck to the small of the back, will never be forgotten. You are caught off guard, embarrassed, and thrilled despite your preparation because the scalpel is so sharp that it unzips the skin rather than cutting it. This exposes the forbidden and hidden sinew underneath. A medical rite of passage and a violation of the sacred, cadaver dissection evokes a wide range of emotions, from disgust, excitement, nausea, annoyance, and amazement to, eventually, the monotony of academic work. Everything hovers between pathos and bathos: here you are, breaking the most basic taboos in society, but you also feel the need for a burrito because formaldehyde is a strong appetite stimulant. The bathos eventually give way as you finish your assignments by slicing open the heart, saw the pelvis in half, and dissect the median nerve. The sacred violation becomes like your typical college class, complete with class clowns, pedants, and the like. For many people, cadaver dissection is the perfect example of how a somber, respectful student can change into a cold, haughty doctor.

My first few days of medical school were extremely serious because of the scope of the moral mission of medicine. It was my second time participating in CPR training, which took place on the first day before we arrived at the cadavers. The first time, back in college, had been ridiculous, unimportant, and everyone was laughing because the plastic mannequins with no limbs and the horribly staged videos were so fake. Now, however, everything was animated by the looming possibility that we might need to use these skills at some point. Along with the jokes of my classmates, I could not help but hear real ribs cracking as I repeatedly slammed my palm into the chest of a tiny plastic child.

The polarity is reversed by cadavers. The cadavers you pretend are fake, and the mannequins you pretend are real. However, you simply cannot on that first day. There was no denying my cadaver's complete humanness and complete death when I looked at him, a little bloated and blue. It seemed inexcusable to me that I would be using a hacksaw to cut this man's head in four months.

However, there are professors of anatomy. Additionally, they advised us to cover our cadaver's face after taking a close look at it because it makes the task easier. We were about to unwrap the head of our cadaver, taking deep breaths and looking earnestly, when a surgeon came by to talk while resting his elbows on the face of the body. He reconstructed the patient's history by pointing out different scars and marks on the bare torso. He most likely died of pancreatic cancer, though there is no scar for that—it killed him too soon. This scar is from an inguinal hernia operation, this one a carotid endarterectomy. These marks here indicate scratching, possibly jaundice, and high bilirubin. In the meantime, I couldn't stop staring at the shifting elbows that rolled over this covered head with every medical theory and vocabulary lesson. I reasoned that prosopagnosia is a neurological condition in which facial vision is impaired. I'd have it, hacksaw in hand, pretty soon.

Because the drama subsided after a few weeks. I found myself emphasizing the macabre, grotesque, and ridiculous in conversations with non-medical students while sharing cadaver stories, seemingly to reassure them that I was normal despite spending six hours a week dissecting a corpse. I would occasionally recount the time I turned around and saw a classmate—the kind of woman with the puffy paint-adorned mug—tiptoeing on a stool, cheerfully driving a chisel into a woman's backbone while splinters flew everywhere. I presented this tale as though to disassociate myself from it, but there was no denying my kinship. After all, hadn't I used a pair of bolt cutters to eagerly disassemble a man's rib cage? When you work with the dead, their humanity comes through even though their faces are hidden and their names are unknown. For example, when I opened the stomach of my cadaver, I discovered two undigested morphine pills, indicating that he had died in agony, possibly by himself and fumbling with a pill bottle cap.

Naturally, the cadavers freely contributed to this fate during their lives, and the language used to describe the bodies in front of us quickly changed to reflect this. We were told that the preferred term was "donors" and that we should no longer refer to them as "cadavers." Indeed, compared to the bad old days, the transgressive aspect of dissection had definitely diminished. For one thing, unlike in the nineteenth century, students were no longer required to bring their own bodies. The OED defines Burke as "to kill secretly by suffocation or strangulation, or for the purpose of selling the victim's body for dissection." Medical schools had also stopped supporting the practice of robbing graves to obtain cadavers, reasoning that it was a vast improvement over murder. However, the most knowledgeable individuals—physicians—rarely gave their bodies. So, how well-informed were the donors? "You wouldn't tell a patient the gory details of a surgery if that would make them not consent," one anatomy professor told me.

Even if donors were sufficiently informed—which they may have been, despite the hesitancy of one anatomy professor—the idea of being dissected wasn't what really frightened them. It was the idea that twenty-two-year-old medical students would rip your parents—your mother, father, and grandparents—to shreds. I kept wondering if this would be the session where I finally puked every time I read the pre-lab and saw a term like "bone saw." Even when I discovered that the "bone saw" in question was actually just a regular, rusty wood saw, I was rarely bothered in the lab. The closest I've ever come to throwing up was on the twentieth anniversary of my grandmother's passing, when I was visiting her grave in New York, far from the lab. I was overcome with emotion, on the verge of tears, and I apologized—not to my corpse, but to its grandchildren. In fact, a son asked for his mother's partially dissected body back in the middle of our lab. She had given her consent, yes, but he couldn't accept that. I knew I would follow suit. (They returned the remains.)

We literally reduced the deceased to organs, tissues, nerves, and muscles in the anatomy lab. You just couldn't deny the corpse's humanity on that first day. However, it was difficult to identify this mass of tissue as human after you had skinned the limbs, cut through awkward muscles, removed the lungs, cut open the heart, and removed a lobe of the liver. It is discomfiting to realize that anatomy lab ultimately becomes more of an interference with happy hour than a violation of the sacred. We were all silently apologizing to our cadavers during our infrequent moments of reflection—not because we felt guilty, but rather because we were unaware of the transgression.

But it was not a straightforward evil. Not just the dissection of cadavers, but all of medicine infringes upon sacred domains. Physicians infiltrate the body in every manner possible. They witness people in their most vulnerable, fearful, and private moments. After escorting them into the world, they retreat. The opposite of alleviating the deepest human suffering is to view the body as matter and mechanism. Conversely, the most severe human suffering is reduced to a simple teaching tool. Even though anatomy professors are at the other end of this spectrum, they still have a connection to the cadavers. Our proctor was both incensed and appalled when I quickly and extensively cut through my donor's diaphragm early on to make it easier to locate the splenic artery. Not because I had ruined a future dissection, misinterpreted a crucial idea, or destroyed an important structure, but rather because I had come across as so careless about it. I learned more about medicine from his expression and his incapacity to express his sorrow than I ever would have from any lecture. Our proctor's sorrow turned to anger when I revealed that another anatomy professor had instructed me to make the cut, and all of a sudden, red-faced professors were being pulled into the hallway.

Kinship was much easier at other times. The professor once questioned, "How old is this fellow?" as he showed us the remnants of our donor's pancreatic cancer.
"Half a dozen," we answered.
He put down the probe, said, "That's my age," and turned to leave.

—

My comprehension of the connection between meaning, life, and death has improved due to medical school. In the doctor-patient relationship, I observed the human relationality I had written about as an undergraduate. As medical students, we were exposed to death, pain, and the labor involved in patient care. But we were also protected from the true weight of accountability, even though we could see its specter. It was simple to view medical school as a simple continuation of undergraduate studies because students spend the first two years in classrooms, where they socialize, study, and read. However, my girlfriend Lucy, who would later become my wife, understood the academic undertones. We had first met during my first year of medical school. I learned from her that her ability to love was hardly limited. While studying the endless wavy lines that comprise an EKG one evening on the sofa in my apartment, she deciphered and correctly identified a deadly arrhythmia. She started crying when she suddenly realized that the patient had not survived, regardless of where this "practice EKG" had come from. The squiggly lines on that page could make you cry because they were more than just lines; they were ventricular fibrillation that was progressing to asystole.

Shep Nuland was still a lecturer at the Yale School of Medicine when Lucy and I were students there, but I only knew him as a reader. How We Die, a famous book about mortality written by renowned surgeon-philosopher Nuland, was published when I was in high school but wasn't until I was in medical school. There weren't many books I'd read that so directly and completely addressed that basic reality of life: everyone dies, whether they are goldfish or grandchildren. I read it at night in my room, and I recall how he described his grandmother's illness in particular, and how that one passage so eloquently showed how the spiritual, medical, and personal all intertwined. When he was younger, Nuland remembered playing a game where he would indent his grandmother's skin with his finger to see how long it took for it to return to its original shape. This was a sign of aging that, along with her newfound dyspnea, demonstrated her "gradual slide into congestive heart failure…the significant decline in the amount of oxygen that aged blood is capable of taking up from the aged tissues of the aged lung." However, he added, "what was most evident was the gradual withdrawal from life." Bubbeh had stopped almost everything else when she stopped praying. When Nuland suffered her fatal stroke, she recalled the words of Sir Thomas Browne's Religio Medici: "We don't know what pains and strife we bring into the world, but it's usually not easy to escape it."

In an effort to gain a deeper understanding of the specifics of death, I had devoted a great deal of time to studying literature at Stanford and medical history at Cambridge, but I still felt as though I didn't fully understand them. I was persuaded that such things could only be known in person by descriptions like Nuland's. To witness the twin mysteries of death, its experiential and biological manifestations—at once intensely personal and completely impersonal—I was studying medicine.

I recall Nuland writing about being a young medical student in the operating room by myself with a patient whose heart had stopped in the first few chapters of How We Die. He attempted to physically squeeze the patient's life back into him by cutting open his chest and manually pumping his heart in a desperate attempt. Nuland was discovered by his supervisor, covered in blood and in failing condition, after the patient died.

By the time I arrived, medical school had evolved to the point where it was simply impossible to imagine such a scene. As medical students, we were hardly permitted to touch patients, much less open their chests. But amid the failure and bloodshed, the heroic spirit of responsibility remained unchanged. This seemed to me to be the ideal representation of a doctor.

—

The first death I saw coincided with the first birth.

I had just completed Step 1 of my medical boards, capping two years of intense study that involved spending time in coffee shops, deep in libraries, buried in books, and reviewing hand-made flash cards while in bed. With patients, not abstractions, as my main focus, I would spend the next two years in the hospital and clinic, finally applying that theoretical knowledge to alleviate tangible suffering. I began working in the labor and delivery ward on the graveyard shift at Ob-Gyn.

I tried to remember the names of the "stations" that marked the baby's descent, the stages of labor, the corresponding dilation of the cervix, and anything else that might be useful when the time came as I walked into the building as the sun was setting. My job as a medical student was to observe and learn without interfering. My main teachers would be nurses, with their years of clinical experience, and residents, who had completed medical school and were now completing training in a chosen specialty. However, the fear persisted—I could sense it fluttering—that I would be asked to give birth on my own and fail, whether by accident or expectation.

To meet the resident, I headed to the doctors' lounge. When I entered, I noticed a young woman with dark hair sitting on a couch, reading a journal article and watching TV, chomping frantically at a sandwich. I gave my introduction.

"Oh, hello," she said. "My name is Melissa. If you need me, I'll be here or in the call room. Monitoring patient Garcia is probably the best course of action for you. This twenty-two-year-old woman has twins and preterm labor. Everyone else is rather typical.

Melissa gave me a flurry of facts and information in between bites: The twins were only twenty-three and a half weeks old; the patient was receiving different medications to manage her contractions; the goal was to continue the pregnancy until the twins were more developed, however long that might be; twenty-four weeks was thought to be the cusp of viability, and every extra day made a difference. Melissa's pager sounded.

She swung her legs off the couch and said, "All right." "I must leave. If you want, you can hang here. Our cable channels are good. Or you could accompany me.

Melissa and I went to the nurses' station together. There were monitors lining one wall with wavy telemetry lines.

"What is that?" I inquired.

That is the result of fetal heartbeat and tachometers. Allow me to introduce the patient to you. She is not fluent in English. Are you fluent in Spanish?

I gave a headshake. Melissa led me to the room. It was gloomy. The twins' heart rates and the mother's contractions were monitored by monitor bands wrapped around her belly as she lay in a bed, sleeping soundly and transmitting the information to the screens I had seen at the nurses' station. With a worried expression on his face, the father stood by the bedside, holding his wife's hand. Melissa escorted me out after whispering something to them in Spanish.

For the next few hours, everything went as planned. Melissa dozed in the living room. After attempting to decipher the unintelligible scrawls in Garcia's chart—which was akin to reading hieroglyphics—I discovered that her first name was Elena, that this was her second pregnancy, that she had not received any prenatal care, and that she lacked insurance. I made a note to look up the names of the medications she was taking later and wrote them down. I came across a textbook in the doctor's lounge that briefly discussed premature labor. If they lived, preemies seemed to have a high incidence of cerebral palsy and brain hemorrhages. However, thirty years prior, my older brother Suman, who was now a practicing neurologist, had been born nearly eight weeks early. I approached the nurse and requested that she show me how to read the tiny squiggles on the monitor, which seemed to predict either peace or catastrophe but were no more readable to me than the doctor's handwriting. She gave me a nod and started explaining how to read a contraction and the fetal heart's response to it. If you looked closely, you could see—

She paused. Her face flashed with concern. She got up without saying anything, rushed into Elena's room, then rushed back outside, picked up the phone, and called Melissa. Melissa showed up a minute later, bleary-eyed, looked at the strips, and hurried into the patient's room, me following. She quickly spoke in a jargon I could only partially understand as she opened her phone and called the attending. I learned that the twins were in distress and that an emergency C-section was their only chance of survival.

They carried me into the operating room with the commotion. With drugs coursing through her veins, they found Elena lying on the table. While the attending, the resident, and I splattered alcohol cleanser on our hands and forearms, a nurse frantically applied an antiseptic solution to the woman's swollen abdomen. I stood silently as they swore under their breath, imitating their urgent strokes. While the attending, the senior surgeon, fidgeted, the anesthesiologists intubated the patient.

"Come on," he said. There isn't much time left. We must go more quickly!

As the attendant cut open the woman's abdomen, I stood beside him. He made a single, long, curvilinear cut just below the apex of her protuberant womb, under her belly button. I searched my mind for anatomical illustrations from textbooks, trying to follow every movement. The touch of the scalpel caused the skin to separate. The first glimpse of the melon-like uterus appeared as he confidently cut through the tough white rectus fascia covering the muscle, then used his hands to split the fascia and the underlying muscle. He also cut that open, revealing a tiny face that vanished in the blood. Like tiny birds dropped too soon from a nest, the doctor's hands plunged in and pulled out one, then two purple babies, barely moving, eyes fused shut. They resembled children's preliminary drawings more than actual children, with their bones showing through their translucent skin. They were passed quickly to the neonatal intensivists who were waiting, who hurried them to the neonatal intensive care unit because they were too small to hold and barely larger than the surgeon's hands.

The operation slowed as the immediate threat was avoided, and the frantic state gave way to something approaching serenity. As tiny blood spurts were stopped by the cautery, the smell of burned flesh rose. The uterus was sutured back together, the stitches biting shut the open wound like a row of teeth.
"Do you want the peritoneum closed, Professor?" Melissa inquired. "I just read that it doesn't have to be."
The attending said, "Let no man tear apart what God has united." "At least only for a short time. Let's sew it back together; I prefer to leave things as I found them.

The membrane that envelops the abdomen is called the peritoneum. I couldn't see it at all now since I somehow missed its opening. Although the wound appeared to me to be a mass of jumbled tissue, the surgeons saw it as having a noticeable order, much like a sculptor would see a block of marble.

Melissa reached into the wound with her forceps, pulled up a clear layer of tissue between the muscle and the uterus, and called for the peritoneal stitch. The peritoneum and the wide hole in it suddenly became visible. After sewing it shut, she used a big needle and several large looping stitches to reassemble the muscle and fascia. After the attendant departed, the skin was eventually sutured together. I was asked to put the final two stitches by Melissa.

As I inserted the needle into the subcutaneous tissue, my hands trembled. I noticed that the needle was a little bent as I tightened the suture. There was a glob of fat showing through the uneven skin.

Melissa let out a sigh. "That's not even," she remarked. "You see this thin white stripe—you just need to catch the dermal layer."

Yes, I did. My eyes would also need to be trained, in addition to my mind.

"Cutters!" The patient was taken to recovery after Melissa removed my amateur knots, resutured the wound, and applied the dressing.

The edge of viability was twenty-four weeks in utero, as Melissa had previously informed me. Twenty-three weeks and six days had passed since the twins' birth. Although their organs were there, they might not have been prepared for the duty of maintaining life just yet. They were entitled to almost four more months of protected development in the womb, where the umbilical cord provided them nutrients and oxygenated blood. The lungs were not equipped to handle the intricate expansion and gas transfer that was respiration, so oxygen would now need to enter through them. Each twin was enclosed in a clear plastic incubator when I visited them in the NICU. They were surrounded by big, beeping machines that were hardly noticeable amidst the maze of tubes and wires. To provide essential human contact, the incubator featured tiny side ports that allowed the parents to reach out and gently stroke a leg or arm.

My shift was over, and the sun had risen. The sight of the twins being taken out of the womb kept me awake as I was sent home. I felt unprepared for the duty of maintaining life, like an immature lung.

I was paired with a new mother when I got back to work that evening. Nobody expected this pregnancy to be problematic. Her actual due date was today, so everything was as normal as possible. I followed the mother's steady progress with the nurse, as her body began to experience increasingly frequent contractions. The cervix dilated from three centimeters to five to ten, the nurse said.

"All right," the nurse said, "it's time to push."

"Don't worry—we'll page you when the delivery is close," she said, turning to face me.

Melissa was in the doctor's lounge when I found her. After a while, the OB team was summoned to the room because the delivery was almost ready. Melissa gave me a gown, gloves, and long boot covers outside the door.

"It becomes a mess," she stated.

We went into the room. Before Melissa shoved me forward, between the patient's legs, directly in front of the attending, I was standing awkwardly off to the side.

"Shuck!" the nurse urged. "Once more: exactly like that, except without the yelling."

The yelling continued, and soon a stream of blood and other liquids followed. Medical diagrams' neatness did nothing to depict nature, which is red in both birth and tooth and claw. (This was not a photo of Anne Geddes.) It was starting to become apparent that becoming a doctor in practice would require a very different education than a medical student in school. Answering multiple-choice questions and reading books had little in common with taking action and the responsibilities that go along with it. It's not enough to know that you should use caution when pulling on the head to help deliver the shoulder. What if I exerted excessive force? (My brain yelled, irreversible nerve damage.) Three steps forward, two steps back, the head emerged with each push and retracted with each pause. I waited. Reproduction, the organism's most fundamental function, has become a perilous endeavor due to the human brain. Labor and delivery units, cardiotoco meters, epidurals, and emergency C-sections were all made possible and required by that same brain.

Uncertain of what to do or when to act, I stood motionless. I gently guided the baby's shoulders as she emerged after the attending voice directed my hands to the emerging head. Easily three times the size of the birdlike creatures from the night before, she was plump, large, and wet. I cut the cord after Melissa clamped it. The child started crying as her eyes opened. After holding the infant for a little while longer to feel her weight and substance, I handed her off to the nurse, who then took her to the mother.

I went outside to the waiting area to share the good news with the extended family. There was a riot of hugs and handshakes as the dozen or so family members who had gathered there leaped to celebrate. I was a prophet who had come down from the top of the mountain to proclaim a happy new covenant! I had just been holding the newest member of this family—this man's niece, this girl's cousin—when all the messiness of the birth vanished.

Ebullient, I returned to the room and met Melissa.

"Hey, how are the twins from last night doing?" I inquired.

She grew darker. Baby B lived for just under twenty-four hours before dying around the time I was giving birth to the new baby, while Baby A died yesterday afternoon. All I could think of at the time was Samuel Beckett and the metaphors that had reached their climax in those twins: "One day we were born, one day we shall die, the same day, the same second...." Birth on top of a grave, the light flashes for a moment, and then it goes dark again. I had been standing beside "the grave digger" while he used his "forceps." How much had these lives been worth?

"You believe that to be bad?" she went on. Most mothers with stillborn children have yet to give birth. Is it possible? These guys had a chance, at least.

A match does not light, but it flickers. The father's lower eyelids' burning red rims, the mother's cries in room 543, and the tears silently streaming down his face: this opposite of happiness, the intolerable, unfair, and sudden presence of death. What words were there for consolation, what sense could be made?

"Was performing an emergency C-section the right decision?" I inquired.

"Without a doubt," she said. "That was their only shot."

"What would happen if you didn't?"

Most likely, they pass away. When the fetal blood becomes academic, the cord is somehow compromised, or something else gravely wrong is occurring, abnormal fetal heart tracings are visible.

However, how can you tell if the tracing is sufficiently poor? Is it worse to be born too early or wait too long to give birth?

"Call for judgment."

It's quite a call. Has I ever had to choose between a harder Reuben and French dip in my life? How could I ever develop the ability to make and accept such decisions? With life and death on the line, would knowledge be sufficient alone? I still had a lot of practical medicine to learn. Surely moral clarity was as important as intelligence. I had to think that somehow I would acquire both knowledge and wisdom. After all, birth and death had only been theoretical ideas when I had entered the hospital the day before. I've seen them both close now. Perhaps Beckett's Pozzo is correct. Perhaps life is just an "instant," too short to think about. However, I would have to concentrate on my impending role as the grave digger with the forceps, closely related to the how and when of death.

My ob-gyn rotation ended soon after, and I moved straight to surgical oncology. I would rotate with another medical student, Mari. After a restless night a few weeks later, she was given the task of helping with a Whipple, a difficult procedure that entails moving the majority of the abdominal organs in an effort to remove pancreatic cancer. During this procedure, a medical student usually stands motionless—or, at most, retracts—for up to nine hours at a time. Due to its extreme complexity—only chief residents are permitted to actively participate—it is regarded as the plum operation to be chosen for assistance. However, it is demanding and the pinnacle of a general surgeon's abilities. I noticed Mari sobbing in the hallway fifteen minutes after the procedure began. Since extensive cancer makes the procedure pointless and necessitates its cancellation, the surgeon always starts a Whipple by passing a tiny camera through a tiny incision to check for metastases. Mari thought in a whisper as she stood in the operating room, waiting with a nine-hour procedure ahead of her: I'm so exhausted—please, God, let there be mets. They were. The procedure was canceled, and the patient was sewn back up. Relief was followed by a growing, gnawing shame. I became a confessor when Mari, in need of one, rushed out of the operating room and saw me.

—

During my fourth year of medical school, I observed as numerous classmates applied for their residencies and chose to specialize in less demanding fields (such as dermatology or radiology). Perplexed by this, I collected data from a number of prestigious medical schools and discovered that the patterns were consistent: by the time they graduated, the majority of students tended to concentrate on "lifestyle" specialties, which include more humane work schedules, higher pay, and less stress, with the idealism of their application essays to medical school tempered or lost. Several students argued that the words "putting our patients' interests above our own" should be removed from our commencement oath, which was a rewriting of the words of Hippocrates, Maimonides, Osler, and a few other great medical forefathers. This was done in keeping with Yale tradition as graduation drew closer. (The rest of us prevented this conversation from going on for very long. The words remained. I found this type of egotism to be completely reasonable and, it should be noted, incompatible with medicine. In fact, 99 percent of people choose their jobs based on factors like pay, hours, and work environment. That's the point, though. You find a job by prioritizing your lifestyle over your calling.)

Personally, I would specialize in neurosurgery. My decision, which I had been considering for a while, was solidified one evening in a room off the operating room when I silently marveled as a pediatric neurosurgeon sat down with the parents of a child who had arrived that evening complaining of headaches and had a large brain tumor. In addition to presenting the clinical facts, he also addressed the human facts, recognizing the tragedy of the circumstance and offering advice. It turned out the child's mother worked as a radiologist. The mother, who had already studied the scans, was devastated as she sat in a plastic chair under fluorescent light, realizing that the tumor appeared to be malignant.

"Now, Claire," said the surgeon quietly.

The mother interrupted, asking if it was as bad as it appeared. "Do you believe it to be cancer?"

"I'm not sure. What I do know—and I know you do, too—is that your life has already changed and will soon change again. You realize that this is going to be a long haul? You must support one another, but you must also take breaks when necessary. This type of illness has the power to unite you or drive you apart. You must support each other now more than ever. Neither of you should spend all night at the patient's bedside or never leave the hospital. Alright?

He continued by outlining the planned operation, the probable results and outcomes, the decisions that needed to be made right away, the decisions that they should begin considering but not make right away, and the kinds of decisions that they shouldn't worry about just yet. The family was still uncomfortable at the end of the talk, but they appeared to be prepared for what lay ahead. Initially wan, dull, and almost otherworldly, I had watched the parents' faces sharpen and focus. As I sat there, it occurred to me that the questions that everyone has at some point about life, death, and meaning typically come up in a medical setting. It turns into a logically philosophical and biological exercise in the real-world scenarios where these questions arise. Since humans are living things, they are governed by physical laws, such as the unfortunate one that states that entropy always rises. The fundamental necessity of life is metabolism, and the end of it is death. Diseases are molecules that are acting inappropriately.

Although all medical professionals treat illnesses, neurosurgeons operate in the furnace of identity because every brain surgery inevitably involves manipulating the essence of who we are, and every discussion with a patient undergoing brain surgery must address this reality. Brain surgery also has the impact of any significant life event because, for the patient and family, it is typically the most dramatic event they have ever experienced. The question at those pivotal moments is not just whether to live or die, but also what kind of life is worthwhile. Would you be willing to give up your mother's or your own speech for a few more months of being silent? The widening of your blind spot for the price of removing the remote chance of a brain hemorrhage that could be fatal? Does your right hand prevent seizures? How much neurological pain would you allow your child to go through before deciding death is better? Since our perception of the world is mediated by the brain, any neurosurgical issue compels a patient and their family to consider what makes life worthwhile enough to continue living, ideally with the assistance of a physician. Neurosurgery's harsh demands for perfection drove me; I believed that virtue necessitated excellence in morals, emotions, intellect, and physical attributes, much like the ancient Greek idea of arete. The most difficult and direct encounter with meaning, identity, and death appeared to be in neurosurgery. Neurosurgeons were experts in a variety of disciplines, including neurosurgery, intensive care unit medicine, neurology, and radiology, in addition to their massive responsibilities. I understood that in addition to training my hands and mind, I would also need to train my eyes and possibly other organs. The thought was overwhelming and enticing. Maybe I could become one of these polymaths who strode into the thickest tangle of spiritual, scientific, and emotional issues and carved out solutions.

Following medical school, Lucy and I got married and moved to California to start our residencies—Lucy at UCSF, and me at Stanford. With medical school officially over, we were ready for the real world. I quickly made a number of close friends at the hospital, especially Jeff, a general surgery resident a few years older than us, and Victoria, my fellow resident. We would progress from watching medical dramas unfold to playing key roles in them over the course of the following seven years of training.

Even though the workload is heavy, an intern in the first year of residency is essentially a paper pusher in a world where lives and deaths are at stake. "Neurosurgery residents aren't just the best surgeons—we're the best doctors in the hospital," the chief resident told me on my first day there. That's what you want. Make us proud. "Always eat with your left hand," the chairman said as he moved through the ward. You must develop your ambidexterity. "Just a heads-up—the chief is going through a divorce, so he's really throwing himself into his work right now," said one of the senior residents. Avoid chit-chatting with him. "The only thing I have to tell you is: they can always hurt you more, but they can't stop the clock," said the departing intern, who was meant to orient me but instead gave me a list of forty-three patients. Then he turned to leave.

For the first two days, I stayed in the hospital, but soon, the seemingly insurmountable, day-killing piles of paperwork were reduced to an hour's work. However, the documents you file while working in a hospital are more than just documents; they are pieces of stories full of struggles and victories. For instance, when eight-year-old Matthew arrived one day complaining of headaches, it was discovered that he had a tumor next to his hypothalamus. Sleep, hunger, thirst, and sex are all basic drives that are controlled by the hypothalamus. If any tumor were left behind, Matthew's childhood would be ruined by radiation therapy, additional surgeries, brain catheterization, etc. That could be avoided by total removal, but doing so runs the risk of harming his hypothalamus and making him a slave to his desires. The surgeon began by drilling off the floor of Matthew's skull and inserting a tiny endoscope through his nose. He removed the tumor after seeing a clear plane inside. A few days later, Matthew was eager to get home and was bouncing around the ward, stealing candies from the nurses. I cheerfully completed the countless pages of his discharge paperwork that evening.

On Tuesday I lost my first patient.

The healthiest person on the general surgery service, where I interned for a month, was a small, trim eighty-two-year-old woman. (The pathologist would be shocked to discover her age at her autopsy: "She has the organs of a fifty-year-old!" She was admitted due to a mild bowel obstruction that causes constipation. We performed a minor operation to help clear her bowels after six days of hoping they would untangle themselves. When I went to check on her Monday night around eight, she was awake and doing well. I took my list of the day's tasks out of my pocket as we were speaking, and I marked off the final item (post-op check, Mrs. Harvey). It was time to return home and rest.

The telephone rang after midnight. The patient was collapsing. I sat up in bed and spat out commands, my complacency from bureaucratic work abruptly gone: "One liter bolus of LR, EKG, chest X-ray, stat—I'm on my way in." When I called my chief, she advised me to add labs and to give her another call when I felt more in control of the situation. Mrs. Harvey was having trouble breathing, her heart was pounding, and her blood pressure was dropping when I hurried to the hospital. No matter what I did, she didn't get better. Since I was the only intern in general surgery on call, my pager was constantly buzzing with calls that I could ignore (patients in the emergency room who needed sleep aids) and ones that I couldn't (a ruptured aortic aneurysm). Mrs. Harvey was still not getting better, and I was drowning, out of my depth, and being pulled in a thousand different directions. After arranging for a transfer to the intensive care unit (ICU), where we administered drugs and fluids to prevent her death, I spent the next few hours alternating between my patient in the emergency room threatening to die and my patient in the ICU actively dying. Mrs. Harvey was comparatively stable at 5:45 a.m., and the ER patient was en route to the operating room. To stay alive, she had required three separate pressors, a ventilator, two units of blood, and twelve liters of fluid.

At five o'clock on Tuesday night, when I eventually left the hospital, Mrs. Harvey was neither improving nor getting worse. The ICU team was trying CPR when the phone rang at seven o'clock. Mrs. Harvey had coded. She made it through again as I hurried back to the hospital. Seldom. This time, I decided to grab dinner close to the hospital just in case, rather than heading home.

Mrs. Harvey had passed away when my phone rang at eight o'clock.

I went to bed at home.

I felt a mixture of sadness and rage. Mrs. Harvey had somehow risen above the tiers of paperwork to become my patient. I went to her autopsy the following day and saw the pathologists dissect her and take out her organs. I examined the knots I had tied in her intestines, ran my hands over them, and looked them over myself. I made the decision to handle all of my paperwork as patients going forward, rather than the other way around.

I would catch a glimpse of my fair share of death during that first year. Sometimes I caught a glimpse of it while skulking around corners, and other times I felt ashamed to be in the same room. Some of the people I witnessed dying were as follows:

1. An alcoholic, his blood no longer able to clot, who bled to death into his joints and under his skin. Every day, the bruises would spread. Before he became delirious, he looked up at me and said, "It's not fair—I've been diluting my drinks with water."
2. A pathologist, dying of pneumonia, wheezing her death rattle before heading down to be autopsied—her final trip to the pathology lab, where she had spent so many years of her life.
3. A man who'd had a minor neurosurgical procedure to treat lightning bolts of pain that were shooting through his face: a tiny drop of liquid cement had been placed on the suspected nerve to keep a vein from pressing on it. A week later, he developed massive headaches. Nearly every test was run, but no diagnosis was ever identified.
4. Dozens of head trauma cases: suicides, gunshots, bar fights, motorcycle accidents, car crashes. A moose attack.

At moments, the weight of it all became palpable. It was air, stress and misery. Normally you inhaled it without noticing it. But some days, like a humid muggy day, it had a suffocating weight of its own. Some days, this is how it felt when I was in the hospital: trapped in an endless jungle summer, wet with sweat, the rain of tears of the families of the dying pouring down.

—

You are the first person to arrive in an emergency during your second year of training. You can't save every patient. Others can: I wandered around the hospital at two in the morning in a euphoric daze until I lost my sense of direction after rushing a comatose patient from the emergency room to the operating room, draining the blood from his skull, and then watching him wake up, begin speaking to his family, and complain about the cut on his head. It took me 45 minutes to figure out how to get out again.

The schedule was a burden. We were putting in up to 100 hours a week as residents, even though the law only allowed us to work eighty-eight hours, there was always more to be done. At two am I drank energy drinks while my headache and my eyes were watering. I was able to maintain my composure at work, but once I left the hospital, I would be overcome by fatigue. Frequently dozing off in my car before making the fifteen-minute drive home to bed, I stumbled through the parking lot.

The strain was too much for some residents to handle. One just couldn't take responsibility or blame. Despite his skill as a surgeon, he was unable to acknowledge his mistakes. One day, he pleaded with me to help him save his career while we were sitting in the lounge.

"You just need to look me in the eye and say, 'I'm sorry,'" I said. I am responsible for what transpired, and I will not allow it to happen again.

" However, the nurse was the one who—

"No. You must be able to say it with sincerity. Try once more.

"But—"

"No. Say it.

Before I realized that he was doomed, this continued for an hour.

Another resident chose to leave the field for a less demanding position in consulting due to stress.

Others would have to pay even more.

My responsibility grew with my skill set. It takes an unachievable prognostic ability to learn to determine whose lives could be saved, whose couldn't be, and whose shouldn't be. I erred. Hurrying a patient to the operating room to preserve just enough of his brain so that his heart beats but he is unable to speak, he must eat through a tube, and he is destined to live a life he would never choose. This, in my opinion, was a more serious failure than the patient's death. Until the inevitable fatal bedsore or pneumonia sets in, the family, unable to find closure, visits the institution less frequently as the twilight existence of unconscious metabolism becomes an intolerable burden. Some people are adamant about this life and are open to the possibility. However, many don't or can't, and the neurosurgeon needs to develop their decision-making skills.

In part, I had begun this career to seek death: to grasp it, to unravel it, to look it in the eye, unblinking. I was drawn to neurosurgery because of the way it intertwines life and death and the brain and consciousness. I had believed that living in the middle would elevate me not just as a platform for acts of compassion but also as a person: removing myself from trivial matters and petty materialism to the core of the issue, to truly life-or-death choices and struggles—certainly a form of transcendence would be found there?

Something else, however, was slowly taking shape in residency. I started to suspect that being so close to the fiery light of such moments only made me blind to their nature, like trying to learn astronomy by staring at the sun, in the middle of this never-ending assault of head injuries. I was only present at those crucial times; I wasn't yet with patients during those times. I saw a great deal of suffering; worse, I grew accustomed to it. One learns to float, swim, and even enjoy life while drowning, even in blood. They also form bonds with the doctors, nurses, and other people who are clinging to the same raft and are caught in the same tide.

Jeff, a fellow resident, and I collaborated on traumas. We were always in sync when he called me down to the trauma bay due to a concomitant head injury. After evaluating the abdomen, he would inquire about my assessment of the patient's cognitive function. I once retorted, "Well, he could still be a senator, but only from a small state." Jeff chuckled, and the state's population became our gauge of the severity of head injuries. "Is he from California or Wyoming?" In an attempt to ascertain the appropriate level of intensity for his care plan, Jeff would inquire. "Jeff, I know his blood pressure is labile, but I have to get him to the operating room or he's going to travel from Washington to Idaho—can you get him stabilized?" is another possibility.

One day, while I was getting my usual lunch in the cafeteria—a sandwich with ice cream and a Diet Coke—my pager announced an impending major trauma. As the paramedics arrived, pushing the gurney and stating the following information, I hurried to the trauma bay, tucking my ice cream sandwich behind a computer. "Twenty-two-year-old male, motorcycle accident, forty miles per hour, possible brain coming out his nose..."

I immediately got to work evaluating his other vital functions and requesting an intubation tray. I examined his numerous wounds, including the dilated pupils, road rash, and bruised face, after he had been safely intubated. He had a broken skull and extensive, diffuse bleeding, so we rushed him to the scanner after pumping him full of mannitol to reduce brain swelling. I was already preparing the scalp incision, including how I would drill the bone and remove the blood. Abruptly, his blood pressure dropped. His heart stopped just as the rest of the trauma team arrived, so we hurried him back to the trauma bay. He was surrounded by a flurry of activity as drugs were pushed into his IVs, catheters were inserted into his femoral arteries, tubes were thrust deep into his chest, and fists were hammered on his heart to maintain the blood flow. We let him die for another half hour. We all whispered to each other that death was preferable to that type of head injury.

Just as the family was being brought in to see the body, I sneaked out of the trauma bay. Then I recalled my ice cream sandwich, my Diet Coke, and the intense heat in the trauma bay. To save the ice cream sandwich in front of the son's corpse, I slipped back in, ghostlike, with one of the emergency room residents filling in for me.

The sandwich was revived after 30 minutes in the freezer. Picking chocolate chips out of my teeth as the family said their final goodbyes, I thought, "Pretty tasty." I questioned whether I had made more moral blunders than progress in my short career as a doctor.

A few days later, I learned that a neurosurgeon had attempted to save Laurie, a friend from medical school, after she was struck by a car. She was revived after coding, but the next day she passed away. I was not interested in learning more. It wasn't long ago when someone was just "killed in a car accident." The images of the gurney roll, the blood on the trauma bay floor, the tube pushed down her throat, and the pounding on her chest all appeared after those words opened a Pandora's box. In addition to hearing the commotion of the drill and smelling the burning bone, its dust swirling, and the crack as I pried off a piece of Laurie's skull, I could also see my hands shaving her scalp and the scalpel slicing open her head. Her head was distorted, and her hair was half-shaven. She didn't look like herself at all; her friends and family didn't recognize her. Perhaps a leg was in traction, and there were chest tubes.

I didn't request specifics. I had too many already.

All of my failed empathy moments suddenly came flooding back to me, including the times I disregarded patients' pain when other demands demanded it and pushed discharge over patient concerns. The people whose pain I witnessed, documented, and neatly bundled into different diagnoses—the importance of which I was blind to—all came back, bitter, irate, and unstoppable.

I worried that I was headed toward becoming Tolstoy's archetype of a doctor, consumed by meaningless formality, devoted to the memorization of illness, and completely oblivious to its greater human significance. "Doctors visited her individually and in consultation, conversed extensively in French, German, and Latin, placed blame on one another, and prescribed a wide range of medications for every illness they were aware of, but none of them ever considered the possibility that they were unaware of the illness Natasha was afflicted with." I was approached by a mother who had just received a brain cancer diagnosis. She was overcome with uncertainty, fear, and confusion. I was worn out and disengaged. I hurried through her inquiries, reassured her that the surgery would go well, and convinced myself that there wasn't enough time to provide her with fair answers. However, why didn't I find the time? For weeks, a stubborn veterinarian disregarded the counsel and encouragement of physicians, nurses, and physical therapists; consequently, his back wound healed exactly as we had forewarned him. He yelled in agony as I stitched the dehiscent wound after calling him out of the operating room and telling myself he had been expecting it.

No one is expecting it.

Richard Selzer and William Carlos Williams had admitted to doing worse, and I vowed to do better, which gave me some small comfort. The significance of human relationships—not between patients and their families, but between a doctor and patient—was something I feared I was losing sight of amid the tragedies and failures. Technical prowess was insufficient. My greatest goal as a resident was to help a patient or family understand death or illness, not to save lives because everyone dies eventually. The initial discussion with a neurosurgeon after a patient has a fatal head bleed may permanently alter the family's memory of the death, turning it from a calm acceptance of death ("Maybe it was his time") to an outward display of regret ("Those doctors didn't listen!"). They never tried to save him. Words are the surgeon's only tool when there is nowhere for the scalpel.

It is not just doctors who fail to recognize the full significance of the unique suffering caused by severe brain damage, which is frequently felt more by families than by patients. Nor, typically, do the families who assemble around their beloved—their beloved whose mutilated heads held bruised brains—realize the full significance. The body in front of them represents the past, the accumulation of memories, and the recently experienced love. I envision the potential futures, the breathing apparatuses attached via a surgical incision in the neck, the gooey fluid seeping in through a hole in the abdomen, and the potential protracted, agonizing, and only partially recovered—or, more frequently, nonexistent—return of the person they remember. I acted as death's ambassador in these situations rather than its enemy, as I usually did. The person they knew—the complete, vital, independent human being—now lived only in the past, and I had to help those families understand that in order to determine what kind of future they would prefer—an easy death or being strung between bags of fluids coming in, others coming out, or persevering despite being unable to struggle—I needed their input.

I might have become a pastor if I had been more devout as a child because that was the pastoral position I had desired.

—

With my renewed focus, informed consent—the process by which a patient signs a document authorizing surgery—became an opportunity to create a covenant with a suffering countryman: Here we are together, and here are the ways through—I promise to guide you, as best as I can, to the other side. It was no longer a legal exercise in listing all the risks as quickly as possible, like the voiceover in a new pharmaceutical advertisement.

I had gained experience and efficiency by this stage of my residency. At last, I was able to take a deep breath and stop clinging to myself. I was now taking full responsibility for my patients' health.

I started thinking about my dad. Lucy and I, as medical students, had gone to his hospital rounds in Kingman and seen how he made his patients feel better and had fun. One woman recuperating from a heart surgery was asked, "Are you hungry? Can I get you something to eat?

"Whatever," she said. "I'm going hungry."

"How about steak and lobster?" Reaching for the telephone, he dialed the nursing station. "My patient needs steak and lobster immediately!" He smiled and turned back to her, saying, "It's on the way, but it might look more like a turkey sandwich."

I was inspired by the trust he established with his patients and the effortless human connections he made.

A terrified-looking 35-year-old sat in her intensive care unit bed. She had a seizure while shopping for her sister's birthday. A benign brain tumor was pressing on her right frontal lobe, according to a scan. It was the best type of tumor to have and the best location for it in terms of operative risk. Surgery would most likely stop her seizures. A lifetime of toxic anti-seizure drugs was the alternative. However, I could see that she was more afraid of brain surgery than most people. She had been swept away from the familiar bustle of a shopping mall and into the unfamiliar beeps, alarms, and antiseptic odors of an intensive care unit, leaving her alone and in an unfamiliar place. If I went into a detached spiel about all the risks and potential complications of surgery, she would probably refuse it. I could take that action, record her refusal in the chart, consider my duty fulfilled, and proceed to the next assignment. Rather, with her consent, I brought her family and we calmly discussed the possibilities. As we conversed, I saw the enormity of the decision she had to make diminish into a challenging yet rational one. She was a person when I first met her, not a problem that needed to be resolved. She decided to have surgery. Everything went without a hitch. Two days later, she returned home and never experienced seizures again.

Any serious illness changes the life of the patient—in fact, the entire family. However, brain disorders also have the esoteric element. How much more unfathomable is it when a patient is brain dead, his body is still warm, and his heart is still beating? The death of a son already defies the parents' ordered universe. There is no better picture to capture the expression on a patient's face when they hear a neurosurgeon's diagnosis: "The root of disaster means a star coming apart." The shock of the news can occasionally cause an electrical short in the brain. This phenomenon, which is a severe form of the swoon some people experience after hearing bad news, is called "psychogenic" syndrome. Upon learning that her father, who had fought for her right to an education in rural 1960s India, had passed away following a protracted hospital stay, my mother, who was alone at college, experienced a psychogenic seizure that persisted until she went back home to attend the funeral. After receiving a brain cancer diagnosis, one of my patients unexpectedly went into a coma. In an attempt to find a cause, I ordered a number of lab tests, scans, and EEGs, but to no avail. The most straightforward test was the one where

I lifted the patient's arm above his face and released it. Just enough willpower is left in a psychogenic coma patient to prevent self-harm. Speaking reassuringly until your words resonate and the patient awakens is the treatment.

There are two types of brain cancer: primary cancers, which originate in the brain, and metastases, which spread from other parts of the body, usually the lungs. Surgery prolongs life but does not cure the disease; for most people, brain cancer indicates death within a year or two. Two days prior, Mrs. Lee, who was in her late fifties and had pale green eyes, had come to my service from a hospital a hundred miles away from her home. Her husband was at her bedside, fidgeting with his wedding ring while wearing a plaid shirt tucked into crisp jeans. After I sat down and introduced myself, she shared her story with me: Her right hand had been tingling for the past few days, and she had started to lose control of it until she was unable to button her blouse. Fearing she was having a stroke, she had visited her local emergency room. She was sent here after an MRI was taken there.

"Has anyone informed you of the results of the MRI?" I inquired.
"No." As was often the case with bad news, the blame had been placed elsewhere. We would frequently argue with the oncologist about who was responsible for breaking the news. How often have I done the same thing? I reasoned that it could end here.
"All right," I replied. "We need to discuss many things." Could you please explain what you understand is going on? Hearing that always helps me to make sure I don't overlook anything.
I was afraid I was having a stroke, but I suppose Am I not?
"That's correct. You're not experiencing a stroke. I stopped. I could see how big the gap was between the life she was going to have and the one she had last week. I took a few steps back because she and her husband didn't seem prepared to hear about brain cancer—is anyone?
"Your symptoms are being caused by a mass in your brain, as revealed by the MRI."

Quiet.

"Are you interested in seeing the MRI?"

"Yes."

To orient her, I pointed to her eyes, ears, and nose as I displayed the pictures on the computer by her bed. I then scrolled up to the tumor, which was a black necrotic core surrounded by a lumpy white ring.

"What is it?" she inquired.

It could be anything. An infection, perhaps. We won't know until after the procedure.

I was still tempted to sidestep the question, to let their apparent concerns drift unchecked in their minds.

I started, "It looks very much like a brain tumor, but we can't be sure until after surgery."

"Is it cancer?"

"Once more, we won't know for sure until our pathologists remove it and examine it, but if I had to guess, I would say yes."

I was convinced by the scan that this was glioblastoma, the most severe form of aggressive brain cancer. However, following Mrs. Lee's and her husband's example, I moved cautiously forward. I didn't think they would remember much else after I brought up the subject of brain cancer. Spoonful was the best way to distribute a tragedy. Most patients needed time to process the information; only a small number demanded it all at once. In contrast to trauma, where you have only ten minutes to explain and make a big decision, they didn't ask about my prognosis, so I was able to calm down. I explained in detail what to expect over the next few days, including what the surgery would entail, how we would only shave a small strip of her hair to keep it looking nice, how her arm would probably become a little weaker afterward but then stronger again, that if everything went well, she would be out of the hospital in three days, that this was just the beginning of a marathon, how important it was to get enough sleep, and that I didn't expect them to remember anything I had just said.

We spoke again after the surgery, this time about the prognosis, radiation, and chemotherapy. I was now familiar with some basic guidelines. First off, the specific figures pertain to research halls rather than hospital rooms. The Kaplan-Meier curve, a commonly used statistic, calculates how many patients survive over time. It is the standard by which we measure advancement and determine the severity of an illness. The curve steeply declines for glioblastoma, with only roughly 5% of patients still alive after two years. Second, accuracy is crucial, but you should always allow for some optimism. I would say, "Most patients live many months to a couple of years," as opposed to, "Median survival is eleven months" or "You have a ninety-five percent chance of being dead in two years." I thought this was a more accurate description. The issue is that it is impossible to predict a patient's exact position on the curve, such as whether she will pass away in six months or sixty. I've come to the conclusion that being more precise than you can be is reckless. Those fictitious physicians who provided precise figures ("The doctor told me I had six months to live"): I wondered who taught them statistics and who they were.

Most patients stay silent when they hear the news. (After all, "one who endures hardship without complaint" is one of the original definitions of the word patient.) Silence usually reigns, whether due to shock or dignity, so holding a patient's hand becomes the means of communication. Some become inflexible right away, usually the spouse instead of the patient: "We're going to fight and beat this thing, Doc." Prayer, wealth, herbs, and stem cells are some of the weapons. That hardness always seems fragile to me, and the only way out of crushing despair is to have unrealistic optimism. In any event, a warlike attitude was appropriate given the urgency of surgery. I was furious in the operating room because the dark gray, decaying tumor appeared to be an intruder in the fleshy peach convolutions of the brain (Got you, you fucker, I muttered). Even though I knew that microscopic cancer cells had already spread throughout that seemingly healthy brain, it was satisfying to remove the tumor. Recurrence was almost inevitable, but that was a problem for another time. Spoonful by spoonful. Being open to human relationality means meeting patients where they are, in the nave or narthex, and bringing them as far as you can. It does not imply revealing grand truths from the apse.

However, there was a cost associated with being receptive to human relationships.

I met Jeff, a friend of mine who works in general surgery, a similarly hard and demanding field, one evening during my third year. Each of us observed the other's dejection. First, you go," he said. And I told how a child who had been so close to making it was shot in the head for wearing shoes of the wrong color. I had hoped that this child would survive the recent wave of deadly, incurable brain tumors, but he had not. I waited for Jeff to tell me his story. "Well, I guess I learned one thing: if I'm ever feeling down about my work, I can always talk to a neurosurgeon to cheer myself up," he said, laughing and punching me in the arm.

Later that evening, as I was driving home, I turned on the radio to listen to NPR's coverage of California's ongoing drought after tactfully informing a mother that her newborn had been born without a brain and would soon pass away. My face started to well up with tears.

There were undoubtedly emotional costs associated with being with patients during these times, but there were also benefits. I don't believe I ever stopped to consider why I was doing this work or if it was worthwhile. Its sacredness made the call to defend life—and not just life, but also another person's identity—perhaps not too much to say about another person's soul.

I came to the realization that I needed to know a patient's identity, values, and what makes his life worthwhile before I could operate on his brain. I also needed to know what destruction would make it reasonable to end that life. My will to succeed came at a heavy price, and I felt almost intolerable guilt over my inevitable failures. One must occasionally be crushed by the weight of carrying another person's cross, which is what makes medicine holy and completely impossible.

—

Additional training time is allocated halfway through the residency. The ethos of neurosurgery—of excellence in everything—maintains that neurosurgery alone is insufficient, which may be unique in medicine. Neurosurgeons must be adventurous and successful in other areas to advance the field. Most of the time, the doctor's focus is on a related field, but occasionally, like with neurosurgeon-journalist Sanjay Gupta, this is very public. The neurosurgeon-neuroscientist path is the most demanding and esteemed.

I started working in a Stanford lab in my fourth year that focused on the development of neural prosthetic technology and basic motor neuroscience, which would enable paralyzed individuals to mentally control a robot arm or computer cursor, for example. Everyone referred to the lab's head, a fellow second-generation Indian professor of electrical engineering and neurobiology, as "V." Despite the fact that V was seven years older than I was, we were like brothers. His lab had established itself as a global leader in brain signal reading, but with his approval, I started a project to write signals into the brain in the opposite direction. After all, you will break a lot of wine glasses if your robot arm is unable to sense how firmly it is grasping one. But the implications of "neuromodulation," or writing signals into the brain, were much broader than that: controlling neural firing could theoretically enable treatment of a variety of neurological and psychiatric conditions that are currently incurable or untreatable, including major depression, Huntington's, schizophrenia, Tourette's, and OCD. The options were endless. I put surgery on hold and started learning how to use novel gene therapy techniques in a number of "first of its kind" experiments.

V and I sat for one of our weekly meetings after I had been there for a year. I had come to enjoy these conversations. Unlike other scientists I knew, V was unique. Soft-spoken and devoted to the clinical mission and people, he frequently confided in me that he wished he had been a surgeon. I discovered that the field of science is as fierce, competitive, and political as it can be, with many opportunities to take shortcuts.

One could rely on V to always make the morally upright (and frequently self-effacing) decision. V argued that our only responsibility was to tell the scientific story honestly and without compromise, while the majority of scientists conspired to get their names out there by publishing in the most prominent journals. I had never encountered someone so prosperous and devoted to morality. V truly was a model citizen.

As I took a seat across from him, he appeared hurt rather than happy. "I need you to put on your doctor's hat right now," he said with a sigh. "All right."

"I have pancreatic cancer, they say."

"All right, V. Tell me the tale.

He described his recent "precautionary" CT scan, which at this point was a truly nonstandard procedure, which revealed a pancreatic mass, his gradual weight loss, and his indigestion. We talked about the future, the dreaded Whipple operation that was imminent ("You will feel like a truck hit you," I told him), the best surgeons, the effects the illness would have on his wife and kids, and how to manage the lab while he was away for an extended period of time. The prognosis for pancreatic cancer is bleak, but naturally, there was no way to know what that meant for V.

He hesitated. "Paul, do you believe that my life is meaningful?" he asked. Did I make the correct decisions?

It was astounding that, in the face of death, even someone I regarded as a model of morality had these doubts.

Although difficult, V's radiation, chemotherapy, and surgery were successful. A year later, as I was starting my clinical responsibilities at the hospital again, he was back at work. His eyes had lost their gleam, and his hair had whitened and thinned. He turned to face me during our last weekly conversation, saying, "You know, today is the first day it seems worth it." Naturally, I would have done anything for my children, but today is the first time that it feels like the pain was worthwhile.

Doctors have a very limited understanding of the hells we put our patients through.

—

My research in V's lab was now limited to days off and idle moments, so I returned to the hospital full-time in my sixth year. The black hole that is neurosurgical residency is not fully understood by most people, including your closest colleagues. One of my favorite nurses told me, "Thank God I have tomorrow off," after staying until ten o'clock one night to assist us in completing a lengthy and challenging case. Do you as well?
"Well, no."
However, you can at least arrive later or something. What time do you typically enter?
"Six A.M."
"No. Really?
"Yes."
"Daily?"
"Daily."

"Even on weekends?"
"Avoid asking."
There's a saying in residency that goes, "The years are short, but the days are long." Depending in part on how quickly you were in the operating room, the day in a neurosurgical residency typically started at six in the morning and ended when the operation was completed.

Technique and speed are used to evaluate a resident's surgical proficiency. Both carelessness and slowness are unacceptable. If you spend too much time being accurate after your first wound closure, the scrub tech will say, "Looks like we've got a plastic surgeon on our hands!" Or: "I understand your plan: the bottom half of the wound will have healed itself by the time you sew the top half! Half the effort— very clever! A junior will be advised by a chief resident to "learn to be fast now." Later you can learn to be good. Everybody's eyes are on the clock in the operating room. For the patient's benefit: How long has he been sedated? Long procedures can cause kidney failure, muscle breakdown, and nerve damage. For the benefit of everyone else, what time do we leave tonight?

I could see that there were two ways to shorten the time, and the tortoise and the hare are probably the best examples of them. The skin opens like a curtain, the skull flap is on the tray before the bone dust settles, and the hare moves as quickly as it can, hands a blur, instruments clattering, and falling to the ground. Because it's not in the best position, the opening may need to be enlarged by a centimeter here or there. Contrariwise, the tortoise moves slowly and methodically, cutting once and measuring twice. Everything proceeds in a precise, systematic manner, so there is no need to go over any of the steps again. The tortoise wins if the hare makes too many small mistakes and has to keep adjusting. The hare prevails if the tortoise takes too long to plan every move.

Whether you move slowly or quickly, the odd thing about time in the operating room is that you don't feel like it's going by. Surgery felt like the opposite of boredom, if boredom is, as Heidegger claimed, the awareness of time passing: the intense focus caused the clock's arms to appear arbitrary. Two hours might seem like just one minute. Normal time abruptly resumed after the last stitch was inserted and the wound was dressed. There was almost a whoosh that could be heard. Then you began to wonder: How long will it take for the patient to wake up? How long does it take to roll in the next case? And what time do I get home tonight?

I didn't notice the length of the day or the drag in my step until the last case was over. Those final administrative duties before being discharged from the hospital felt like anvils.
Will it be able to wait until tomorrow?
No.
With a sigh, Earth resumed its rotation towards the sun.

—

I was responsible for almost everything as a chief resident, and I had more chances than ever to succeed—or fail. I realized that technical excellence was a moral necessity after experiencing the agony of failure. Good intentions weren't enough when so much hinged on my abilities and there was only a millimeter or two separating triumph from tragedy.

The young child with the brain tumor who had enchanted the ward a few years prior, Matthew, was readmitted one day. The operation to remove his tumor had actually caused some minor damage to his hypothalamus, turning the cute eight-year-old into a twelve-year-old monster. He had violent outbursts and never stopped eating. Purple scratches left scars on his mother's arms. Matthew was eventually placed in an institution because he had turned into a demon that could be called upon by a single millimeter of damage. Even though a surgeon and a family jointly determine that the advantages of a surgery outweigh the risks, this was still devastating. Nobody wanted to imagine Matthew as a twenty-year-old who weighed three hundred pounds.
On a different day, I treated a Parkinson's tremor by inserting an electrode nine centimeters deep into the patient's brain. The subthalamic nucleus, a small almond-shaped structure located deep within the brain, was the target. Its various components serve distinct purposes, including movement, emotion, and cognition. We activated

the operating room current to measure tremors. We all agreed that the patient's left hand appeared to have less tremor after focusing on it.

The patient's perplexed voice then broke through our affirmative mutterings: "I feel overwhelmingly sad."

"Now off!" I exclaimed.

The patient remarked, "Oh, the feeling is going away now."

"All right, let's check the impedance and current again. All right. Presently on...

"No, everything... It's just so depressing. It's simply gloomy and depressing.

"The electrode is out!"

After removing it, we put the electrode back in, this time two millimeters to the right. The shaking stopped. Fortunately, the patient was feeling well.

I once worked on a late-night case involving a suboccipital craniectomy for a brain-stem malformation with a neurosurgery attending. Even if you have a lot of experience, it can be challenging to get to the most difficult part of the body for one of the most elegant surgeries. However, I experienced fluidity that night: the instruments felt like extensions of my fingers; the bone, muscle, and skin all seemed to unzip themselves; and I found myself gazing at a thick mass deep within the brainstem that was glistening and yellow. The attendant abruptly stopped me.

"Paul, what would happen if you made a two-millimeter cut here?" He gestured.

My mind was racing with neuroanatomy slides.

"Two eyes?"

"No," he replied. The term "locked-in syndrome" With the exception of blinking, the patient would be totally paralyzed after another two millimeters. He kept his eyes on the microscope. "And I know this because that's exactly what happened the third time I performed this operation."

Neurosurgery necessitates a dedication to both one's own excellence and another's identity. In addition to evaluating one's skills, the decision to operate at all requires a thorough understanding of the patient and her values. Affected body parts become paralyzed when damage occurs to certain brain regions, such as the primary motor cortex, which are thought to be nearly inviolable. However, the areas of the cortex that govern language are the most sacred. Wernicke's and Broca's areas are typically found on the left side and are used for language comprehension and production, respectively. When Broca's area is damaged, the patient can understand language easily but is unable to write or speak. Wernicke's area damage impairs language comprehension; the patient can still speak, but her language is a stream of disconnected words, phrases, and images—a grammar devoid of semantics. The patient becomes isolated and loses something essential to her humanity if both areas are harmed. The destruction of these areas after a stroke or head trauma frequently inhibits the surgeon's desire to save a life: Without language, what sort of life is there?

The first patient I encountered with this kind of issue as a medical student was a sixty-two-year-old man who had a brain tumor. "Mr. Michaels, how are you feeling today?" the resident asked him as we walked into his room during morning rounds.
"Four six one eight nineteen!" was his somewhat amicable response.
He could only speak in numerical sequences due to the tumor's disruption of his speech circuitry, but he retained his prosody and his ability to emote, including sighing, frowning, and smiling. He rattled off another set of numbers, more quickly this time. He had something he wanted to tell us, but the numbers could only convey his anger and fear. For some reason, I stayed in the room while the team got ready to leave.
Holding my hand, he begged me, "Fourteen one two eight." The words "fourteen one two eight"

"I apologize."

"Fourteen one two eight," he said somberly as he looked directly into my eyes.

After that, I departed to rejoin the team. A few months later, he died and was buried with whatever message he wanted the world to know. The surgeon takes many precautions, ordering a variety of scans and a thorough neuropsychological evaluation when tumors or malformations border these language areas. However, the patient is awake and conversing during the procedure. The surgeon uses a handheld ball-tip electrode to deliver electrical current to a small area of the cortex after the brain is exposed, but before the tumor is removed. The patient then performs various verbal tasks, such as reciting the alphabet or naming objects. The patient's speech is disrupted when the electrode delivers current to a crucial area of the cortex: "A B C D E guh guh guh rrrr… F G H I. In order to map the brain and the tumor and determine what can be safely removed, the patient is kept awake the entire time while engaging in a mix of small talk and formal verbal tasks.

While preparing for one of these cases one evening, I looked over the patient's MRI and saw that the language areas were entirely covered by the tumor. Not encouraging. After going over the notes, I discovered that the case had been judged too risky for surgery by the hospital's tumor board, which is composed of a team of highly qualified surgeons, oncologists, radiologists, and pathologists. What other course of action might the surgeon have taken? I felt a little offended because it was our responsibility to say no at some point. They wheeled the patient into the room. He pointed to his head while maintaining eye contact with me. "This thing needs to be removed from my fucking brain." Do you understand?

When the attendant walked in, she noticed my facial expression. "I understand," he said. I spent roughly two hours trying to talk him out of this. Do not bother. All set to go?

Throughout the procedure, we were subjected to a barrage of expletives and encouragement in place of the customary alphabet recital or counting exercise.

"Has that fucking thing left my mind already? What's causing you to slow down? Move more quickly! I want it to go. I don't care if I spend the entire day here; just get it out!

I carefully removed the massive tumor, paying close attention to the smallest sign of speech problems. The tumor now sat on a petri dish, the patient's clean brain shining, his monologue unabated.

"What made you stop? Are you some sort of jerk? I told you I wanted to get rid of the fucking thing.

"It's finished," I declared. "It's out."

How did he continue to speak? It didn't seem possible, considering the tumor's size and location. The rest of language was said to function on a slightly different circuit than profanity. Maybe his brain had been rewired in some way by the tumor.

However, the skull was not going to shut on its own. Tomorrow will be time to speculate.

—

I was at the highest level of my residency. I was a fundamentals expert. The greatest honors had gone to my research. People from all over the nation were showing interest in the job. Stanford began looking for a neurosurgeon-neuroscientist with expertise in neural modulation techniques, a role that perfectly matched my interests. "I just heard from the bosses—if they hire you, you're going to be my faculty mentor!" said one of my junior residents.

I said, "Shhhh." "Avoid jinxing it."

I had the impression that the disparate threads of biology, morality, life, and death were at last starting to come together to form a cohesive worldview and a sense of my role within it, if not an ideal moral code. In highly charged fields, doctors met patients at the most authentic moments when life and identity were in danger. It was their responsibility to find out what made that patient's life worthwhile and, if that was impossible, to plan to allow them to die peacefully. Such authority came with a great deal of responsibility, including guilt and recrimination.

My phone rang while I was in San Diego attending a conference. My roommate, Victoria.

"Paul?"

There was a problem. My stomach grew constricted.

"What's going on?" "I said."

Quiet.

"Vic?"

It's Jeff. He took his own life.

"What?"

We had lost contact because Jeff was completing his surgical fellowship in the Midwest and we were both extremely busy. I tried, but was unable, to remember our last conversation.

"Apparently, he had a challenging complication, and his patient passed away." He scaled a building's roof last night and leaped from it. Other than that, I don't really know anything.

I searched for a question that would help people understand. There was none to be found. I could only imagine the tidal wave of guilt that had carried him off that building and up.

I fervently hoped that I could have been with him as we left the hospital that night. I wish we could have expressed our sympathy the way we used to. If only to get his shrewd, astute advice, I wished I could have shared with Jeff what I had learned about life and our chosen path. Death is inevitable for everyone. As living, breathing, metabolizing beings, it is our destiny, and that of our patients. Death is what happens to you and those around you. Most people live their lives passively. However, Jeff and I had spent years learning how to actively confront death, to wrestle with it, as Jacob did with the angel, and to do so to face the purpose of life. We had taken on the burden of mortal responsibility, which was a heavy burden. Even though we have control over our patients' identities and lives, death always prevails. The world isn't perfect, even if you are. The key is to struggle to win for your patients even though you know that the odds are stacked against you, that you will lose, and that your hands or judgment will slip. Perfection is unachievable, but you can believe in an asymptote you should aim for constantly.

PART 2
Cease Not till Death

If I were a writer of books, I would compile a register, with a comment, of the various deaths of men: he who should teach men to die would at the same time teach them to live.

—Michel de Montaigne, "That to Study Philosophy Is to Learn to Die"

LYING NEXT TO LUCY That identity as a doctor—my identity—no longer mattered in the hospital bed, while we were both crying and the CT scan images were still glowing on the computer screen. The diagnosis was obvious because the cancer had spread to several organ systems. There was silence in the room. Lucy declared her love for me. I said, "I don't want to die." I told her to get married again because I couldn't stand the idea of her being by herself. I advised her that we promptly refinance the mortgage. We began phoning relatives. We talked about the scan and the anticipated future treatments when Victoria eventually stopped by the room. I interrupted her when she mentioned the practicalities of going back to residency.

"Victoria," I declared, "I will never return as a physician to this hospital." Do you not think so?

My life seemed to have ended. Maybe the entire book was coming to an end. I was the sheep, lost and bewildered, rather than the shepherd facilitating a life transition. Serious illness was life-shattering rather than life-altering. It felt more like someone had just firebombed the way ahead than like an epiphany—a sharp flash of light illuminating What Really Matters. I'd have to get around it now.

Jeevan, my brother, was at my bedside. "You've done so much," he remarked. "Don't you know that?"

I let out a sigh. The words sounded hollow, but he meant well. Potential that would now remain unfulfilled had been built throughout my life. I had so much planned, and I had almost done it. My personal identity and imagined future crumbled, I was physically disabled, and I experienced the same existential dilemmas as my patients. The diagnosis of lung cancer was verified. My hard-won, meticulously planned future was gone. Death, whom I knew so well from my work, was now making an in-person appearance. Even though we were finally meeting in person, nothing about it felt familiar. As if a sandstorm had wiped out all traces of familiarity, I stood at the intersection where I should have been able to see and follow the footprints of the innumerable patients I had treated over the years, but instead I saw only a blank, a harsh, vacant, gleaming white desert.

The sun was going down. My discharge was scheduled for the following morning. The nurse informed me that my oncologist would visit that evening before departing to pick up her children, even though we had an oncology appointment scheduled for later in the week. Emma Hayward wanted to introduce herself before the first office visit. Although I had previously treated some of Emma's patients, we had never spoken beyond polite professional exchanges. Lucy sat by the bed and held my hand while my brothers and parents were strewn about the room, silent. Her white coat was worn from a long day, but her smile was still bright as she entered through the open door. Her fellow and a resident followed in her wake. Emma, who was only a few years older than me, had long, dark hair that was streaked with gray, as is typical of anyone who spends time with death. She pulled up a chair.

"Hello, I'm Emma," she said. "I apologize for having to be so brief today, but I wanted to stop by and say hello."
My arm was caught in the IV line as we shook hands.
I said, "Thanks for coming by." "I am aware that you have children to pick up. This is my family. She greeted Lucy, my brothers, and my parents with a nod.
She said, "I'm sorry this is happening to you." "To everyone. In a few days, there will be plenty of time for conversation. To help direct

treatment, I went ahead and had the lab begin performing some tests on your tumor sample. Depending on the results of the tests, chemotherapy may or may not be used as treatment.

I had been hospitalized for appendicitis eighteen months prior. After that, I was treated more like a colleague than a patient—almost like a consultant in my own case. Here, I anticipated the same thing. I continued, "I know this isn't the right time, but I would like to discuss the Kaplan-Meier survival curves."

"No," she replied. "Definitely not."

A moment of quiet. How could she? I pondered. This is how physicians, including myself, understand prognostication. I'm entitled to know.

She said, "We can discuss therapies later." If you would like to, we can also discuss your returning to work. Because you are a surgeon, we would likely substitute carboplatin for cisplatin, which will better protect your nerves. The traditional chemotherapy combination of cisplatin, pemetrexed, and possibly Avastin also has a high rate of peripheral neuropathy.

Return to your job? What is she discussing? Does she have hallucinations? Or have I miscalculated my prognosis? And without a reasonable survival estimate, how can we discuss any of this? The ground roiled and buckled once more, as it had in the previous days.

She went on, "I know this is a lot to take in, so we can work on the specifics later." I mainly wanted to get to know everyone before our Thursday appointment. Apart from survival curves, is there anything else I can do or answer today?

"No," I replied, my head spinning. "I really appreciate you coming by. Thank you so much.

"This is my card," she said, "and the clinic number is on it. Before we see you in two days, don't hesitate to call if something comes up.

My friends and family immediately contacted our network of medical colleagues to identify the top lung cancer oncologists in the nation. Was it appropriate for me to receive treatment at the major cancer centers in Houston and New York? We could deal with the logistics of moving, temporarily relocating, or whatever later. The responses were prompt and largely in agreement: As a world-renowned oncologist and the lung cancer expert on one of the major national cancer advisory boards, Emma was not only one of the best but also a compassionate person who knew when to push and when to back off. I pondered for a moment the series of events that had sent me circling the globe, my residency decided by a computerized matchmaking process, only to find myself here, with a strange diagnosis, under the care of one of the best medical professionals to treat it.

As the cancer progressed, I had become noticeably weaker after spending the majority of the week in bed. The identity associated with my body had drastically changed. Getting in and out of bed to use the restroom required planning and effort and was no longer an automated subcortical motor program. The physical therapists left me a list of supplies to help me get home, including a modified toilet seat, a cane, and foam blocks to support my legs when I'm sleeping. Numerous novel painkillers were recommended. As I limped out of the hospital, I pondered how I had been in the operating room for almost thirty-six hours in a row only six days prior. In a week, had I become that much sicker? In part, yes. However, to survive those thirty-six hours, I also employed a variety of strategies and the assistance of fellow surgeons. Nevertheless, I still endured terrible pain. Had my fears been validated by the CT scan and the lab results, which revealed not just cancer but a body overtaken and on the verge of death, freed me from my obligations to help others, to neurosurgery, to the pursuit of goodness, and to serve patients? Yes, I thought, and therein lay the paradox: without that obligation to care for the sick pushing me forward, I became an invalid, like a runner who crosses the finish line only to collapse.

Usually, when I had a patient with an odd ailment, I read up on it and spoke with the appropriate specialist. This appeared to be the same, but as I began reading about chemotherapy—which involved a wide range of agents—and a host of more recent, innovative treatments that focused on particular mutations, the sheer volume of questions I had hindered any fruitful directed research. "A little learning is a dangerous thing; / Drink deeply, or taste not the Pierian spring," said Alexander Pope. I was unable to locate myself on the Kaplan-Meier curve and integrate myself into this new informational environment without the necessary medical experience. I eagerly awaited my appointment at the clinic.

I mostly rested, though.

I sat looking at a picture of Lucy and me from medical school, laughing and dancing. It was very depressing to see those two arranging their lives together without realizing how fragile they were. Was this any more cruel than when my friend Laurie lost her fiancé in a car accident?

To change my life from that of a doctor to that of a patient, my family got really busy. To help ease the excruciating back pain, we purchased an ergonomic mattress, ordered a bed rail, and opened an account with a mail-order pharmacy. Our financial plan, which had been based on my income doubling sixfold over the next year, now appeared to be in jeopardy. A number of new financial tools appeared to be required to safeguard Lucy. In his words, "I was going to beat this thing, I would somehow be cured," my father said that these changes were a surrender to the illness. How many times had I heard a member of a patient's family make similar claims? At the time, I was unsure of how to respond to them, and now, I was unsure of how to respond to my father.

What was the other story?

—

Lucy and I met Emma at the clinic two days later. In the waiting area, my parents lingered. Paramedics took my vitals. Emma pulled up a chair in front of me so we could speak face-to-face and eye-to-eye. She and her nurse practitioner were remarkably punctual.

"Hello once more," she said. "This is my right hand, Alexis." She pointed to the NP, who was taking notes at the computer. "I know we have a lot to talk about, but let me start by asking how you're doing."

"All right," I said, taking everything into account. Having fun on my 'vacation,' I suppose. How are you?

"Oh, I'm all right." Patients don't usually inquire about their doctors' well-being, but Emma was a coworker, so she paused. "You understand that I am in charge of the inpatient service this week." She grinned. Lucy and I were aware. Periodically, outpatient specialists would rotate on the inpatient service, adding several hours of work to an already busy day.

Following additional introductions, we had a relaxed conversation about the current status of lung cancer research. She said there are two ways to proceed. Chemotherapy was the conventional approach, which broadly targeted rapidly dividing cells, including those found in your intestines, hair follicles, bone marrow, and other organs. As if speaking to another physician, Emma went over the information and choices, again avoiding any reference to Kaplan-Meier survival curves. However, more recent treatments had been created that focused on particular molecular flaws in the cancer. I was shocked to learn how much progress had been made in these efforts, which I had heard about because they had long been considered the holy grail of cancer research. It appeared that "some" patients had long-term survival as a result of these treatments.

Emma said, "The majority of your tests are back." Nobody is certain what your PI3K mutation means just yet. There is still no test for EGFR, the most prevalent mutation in patients like you. That's probably what you have, and if so, you can take a medication called Tarceva in place of chemotherapy. You're so sick that I've scheduled you for chemotherapy beginning on Monday in case the EGFR test comes back negative, even though that result should be back tomorrow, Friday.

I sensed kinship right away. I approached neurosurgery this way. Always have a plan A, B, and C. Our primary choice for chemotherapy will be between carboplatin and cisplatin. Head-to-head, carboplatin is better tolerated in isolated studies. Although all of the data is outdated and there is no direct comparison with our current chemotherapy regimens, cisplatin may have better results but much worse toxicity, particularly for the nerves. What are your thoughts?

I remarked, "I'm not as concerned about protecting my hands for surgery." I have many things I can do with my life. I can find another job or choose not to work if I lose my hands.

She hesitated. "I would like to know if you think surgery is important. Would you like to engage?

"Yes, I have prepared for it for nearly a third of my life."

"All right, then I'll recommend that we continue using carboplatin. It might significantly alter your quality of life, but I don't think it will alter survival. Do you have any more inquiries?

I was happy to follow her since it seemed obvious that this was the right course of action. Perhaps, I started to convince myself, I could do surgery once more. I noticed a slight relaxation in myself.

"Am I allowed to start smoking?" I made a joke.

Emma rolled her eyes as Lucy laughed.

"No. Are there any important inquiries?

"The Kaplan-Meier—"

"We're not talking about that," she stated.

Her resistance was incomprehensible to me. I was a doctor, after all, and I knew these figures. I would have to do that since I could look them up on my own.

"All right," I replied, "then I believe everything is fairly obvious. You will update us on the EGFR results tomorrow. If so, we'll begin taking Tarceva. If not, Monday is when we begin chemotherapy.

"All right. I also want to let you know that I am now your doctor. You should come to us first for any issue, whether it be primary care or something else entirely.

I had a twinge of kinship again.

"Thank you," I replied. "I hope the inpatient wards go well."

She popped her head back in a second after leaving the room. "There are some lung cancer fundraisers who would love to meet you, but feel free to decline. Give it some thought before responding, and then let Alexis know if you think you might be interested. Avoid doing things you don't want to do.

"She's great," Lucy said as we were leaving. You're a good match for her. However... She grinned. "She seems to like you."

"And?"

"Well, according to a study, physicians who have a personal stake in a patient's outcome perform worse at prognostication."

"I think that's in the bottom quartile on our list of things to worry about," I said, laughing.

I started to see that nothing and everything had changed due to my intense encounter with my own mortality. I knew I would die someday, but I had no idea when, until my cancer was discovered. I knew I would die eventually after receiving the diagnosis, but I was unsure of when. But I was acutely aware of it now. It wasn't really a scientific problem. Death is an unsettling fact. There is no other way to live.

—

The medical mist was gradually dissipating; at least I now knew enough to start reading the literature. Although the exact figures were not clear, it appeared that having an EGFR mutation increased life expectancy by about a year on average, with the possibility of long-term survival; not having it indicated an 80 percent chance of dying within two years. It was going to take some time to make sense of the rest of my life.

Lucy and I visited the sperm bank the following day to preserve gametes and options. At the conclusion of my residency, we had always intended to have children, but now We would have to freeze sperm before I began treatment because the cancer medications would have an unidentified effect on my sperm. A young woman showed us various payment plans, storage options, and legal ownership forms. Numerous vibrant pamphlets about different social events for young people with cancer, such as open-mike nights, improv groups, and a cappella groups, were scattered across her desk. Knowing that they all most likely had highly treatable cancers and reasonable life expectancies, I envied their joyful expressions. Lung cancer only affects 0.0012% of people over 36. Yes, everyone who has cancer is unlucky, but there are two types of cancer: cancer and CANCER. To have the latter, you have to be extremely unlucky. Lucy started crying when she asked us to specify what would happen to the sperm if one of us "were to die"—who would legally own them in that case.

About a thousand years ago, the word "hope" first appeared in English, signifying a mix of desire and confidence. However, death was what I was certain of, not what I wanted—life. Did I truly mean to say, "Leave some room for unfounded desire," when I spoke of hope? No. Medical statistics use tools like confidence levels, confidence intervals, and confidence bounds to quantify our confidence in our data in addition to describing numerical values like mean survival. "Leave some room for a statistically unlikely but plausible outcome— a survival just above the measured 95 percent confidence interval," is what I meant to say. Was hope like that? Is it possible to separate the curve into existential segments, such as "defeated," "pessimistic," "realistic," "hopeful," and "delusional"? The numbers were just numbers, weren't they? Had we all simply succumbed to the "hope" that each patient was exceptional?

Once I became a statistician, I realised my relationship with statistics had changed.
I had sat with innumerable patients and their families during my residency to discuss dire prognosis; it's one of the most significant tasks a doctor can perform. When a patient has a severe brain bleed and is ninety-four years old and in the final stages of dementia, it is

easier. However, there aren't really any words for someone like me, a thirty-six-year-old who has been told that their cancer is terminal.

It's not just that they are unable to provide patients with precise prognoses. Indeed, doctors are tasked with bringing a patient's expectations within the range of reasonable possibility if they are significantly beyond the bounds of probability—for example, expecting to live to 130 or believing that a benign skin spot is an indication of impending death. Patients are looking for existential authenticity, which each person must discover for themselves, not scientific knowledge that doctors conceal. It is like trying to quench a thirst with salty water when you delve too deeply into statistics. There is probably no cure for the anxiety that comes with facing death.

I received a call confirming that I did, in fact, have a treatable mutation (EGFR) after we got home from the sperm bank. Fortunately, the chemotherapy was stopped, and I started taking a small white pill called Tarceva. I quickly started to feel more resilient. And I sensed it—a glimmer of hope— although I no longer truly understood what it was. A sliver of blue sky broke through the fog that surrounded my life, and it rolled back another inch. My appetite returned in the ensuing weeks. I gained some weight. I got the typical severe acne that goes hand-in-hand with a positive reaction. My smooth skin, which Lucy had always admired, was now pockmarked and bleeding profusely from my blood thinners. To be fair, I was glad to be alive and ugly, but any aspect of myself that was associated with being handsome was gradually being erased. Lucy claimed to still love my skin despite my acne, but I was experiencing its embodied nature even though I knew that our identities come from more than just the brain. I was no longer the man who threw his laughing niece high in the air, who loved hiking, camping, and running, and who showed his love with giant hugs. I could try to be him again, at most.

Emma and I talked about everything from the medical ("How's the rash?") to the more existential during our first of many biweekly appointments. One possibility was the conventional cancer narrative, which advised putting one's toes in the peat, spending time with family, and regressing.

"After receiving a diagnosis, many people completely stop working," she said. Others pay close attention. Either way, it's acceptable.

"I had planned my entire forty-year career, spending the first twenty years as a surgeon-scientist and the final twenty years as a writer. I'm probably in my last twenty years now, but I'm not sure what career path I should take.

She replied, "Well, I can't tell you that." "All I can say is that you have to decide what matters most to you, but you can return to surgery if you want to."

It would be simpler if I knew how much time I had left. I would write if I had two years. I would return to science and surgery if I had ten.

"I can't give you a number, you know."

Yes, I was aware. As she often said, it was up to me to discover what my values were. A part of me thought this was a cop-out: all right, so I never gave patients exact numbers either, but didn't I always have an idea of how they would fare? How else did I decide what was right and wrong? Then I remembered my mistakes, like the time I advised a family to remove their son's life support, only to have the parents come two years later to show me a YouTube video of him playing the piano and to thank me for saving his life by bringing cupcakes.

The most significant of my numerous new appointments with various medical professionals was with my oncologist, but they weren't the only ones. We started seeing a couples therapist who specializes in cancer patients at Lucy's insistence. Lucy and I sat in side-by-side armchairs in her windowless office and talked about how my diagnosis had broken our lives, both now and in the future. We talked about the pain of knowing and not knowing the future, the challenge of making plans, and the need to support one another. Actually, our marriage had been saved by cancer.

At the conclusion of our first session, the therapist remarked, "Well, you two are coping with this better than any couple I've seen." "I'm not sure if I can offer you any advice."

As we left, I chuckled because, at least, I was doing something well once more. The years of caring for patients who were near death had paid off! I thought Lucy would smile when I turned to face her, but she was just shaking her head.

She took my hand in hers and said, "Don't you get it?" "It doesn't get better than this if we're the best at it."

Does the burden of mortality at least become more familiar if it doesn't get lighter?

I started to see the world from two different angles after receiving a terminal illness diagnosis; I was beginning to see death as both a patient and a doctor. As a physician, I knew better than to say, "Cancer is a battle I'm going to win!" or to wonder, "Why me?" (Reply: Why don't I?) I was well-versed in medical care, complications, and algorithms for treatment. Like AIDS in the late 1980s, stage IV lung cancer is still a disease that kills people quickly, but new treatments are giving people years of life for the first time. This is what I quickly learned from my oncologist and my own research.

It didn't help me as a patient, even though my training as a doctor and scientist had helped me process the information and accept the limitations of what it might show about my prognosis. It didn't explain to Lucy and me what it meant to raise a child while my own life waned or whether we should proceed with having one. It also didn't tell me if I should fight for my career or reclaim the goals I had so steadfastly pursued for so long, but I didn't know if I would have the time to accomplish them.

I needed Emma's assistance to confront my mortality and try to figure out what made my life worthwhile, just like I do with my own patients. I struggled to rebuild my old life—or perhaps find a new one—while facing my own death, torn between being a patient and a doctor, exploring medical science and returning to literature for answers.

—

I spent most of my week in physical therapy rather than cognitive therapy. Almost all my patients had been sent for physiotherapy. And now I was astounded by how challenging it was. You understand what it's like to be ill as a doctor, but you can't truly understand until you've experienced it yourself. It's like having a child or falling in love. You don't value the small things or the mountains of paperwork that accompany it. For instance, when an IV is inserted, you can taste the salt as soon as the infusion begins. I've been in medicine for eleven years, and they tell me that everyone experiences this, but I had no idea.

I was only lifting my legs in physical therapy; I wasn't even using weights yet. It was humiliating and exhausting. Although my brain was functioning normally, I didn't feel like myself. The person who could run half marathons was a faint memory, and my body was weak and fragile. This also shapes who you are. An identity can be shaped by back pain, exhaustion, and nausea. My PT, Karen, inquired about my objectives. I decided to go for a run and bike. In the face of weakness, determination set in. I persisted day after day, and each little boost in strength expanded the range of potential worlds and me. I began to push myself to the limit during my workouts by increasing the number of reps, weights, and minutes. I was able to sit for thirty minutes without getting tired after two months. I could resume having dinner with my friends.

Lucy and I took a car down to our favorite riding route, Cañada Road, one afternoon. (I must add out of pride that we usually rode our bikes there, but the hills were still too steep for my frail frame.) I made it through six shaky miles. It was a far cry from the breezy, thirty-mile rides of the previous summer, but at least I could balance on two wheels.

Was it win or lose?

I started looking forward to meeting Emma. I felt like myself, like a self, in her office. I had lost my identity outside her office. I didn't feel like myself because I wasn't working. I was a neurosurgeon, a scientist, and a young man with a promising future ahead of him. At home, crippled, I worried that I wasn't a good husband to Lucy. In every sentence of my life, I had moved from the subject to the direct object. In fourteenth-century philosophy, the word patient simply meant "the object of an action," and I felt like one. As a doctor, I was an agent, a cause. As a patient, I was just something that happened. But in Emma's office, Lucy and I could joke, trade doctor lingo, talk freely about our hopes and dreams, and try to assemble a plan to move forward. Two months in, Emma remained vague about any prognostication. Every statistic I cited she rebuffed with a reminder to focus on my values. Though I felt dissatisfied, at least I felt like somebody, a person, rather than a thing exemplifying the second law of thermodynamics (all order tends toward entropy, decay, etc.).

Flush in the face of mortality, many decisions became compressed, urgent and non receding. Foremost among them for us: Should Lucy and I have a child? We had always been deeply in love, although our marriage had been tense near the end of my residency. We still had a deep and developing vocabulary about what was important in our relationship. We believed that raising children added another dimension to meaning, if human relations were the foundation of meaning. We both felt compelled by instinct to add another chair to our family's table, even though it had always been something we had desired.

We both thought of each other, we both wanted to be parents. Although Lucy hoped I had years left, she felt that I should make the decision about whether or not to spend my remaining time as a father after learning my prognosis.

One night while we were lying in bed, she asked me, "What do you feel most sad or afraid about?"
I told her, "I'm leaving you."

I was certain that Lucy should make the final decision because she would probably have to raise the child alone and take care of us both as my illness worsened. I knew that having a child would make the whole family happier, and I couldn't bear to think of Lucy being husbandless and childless after I passed away.

She questioned, "Will having a newborn take away from our time together?" "Don't you think it will be more painful to die if you say goodbye to your child?"

"It would be fantastic if it did," I remarked. Both Lucy and I believed that avoiding pain was not life's purpose.

I realized years ago that Nietzsche and Darwin shared a common belief: the organism's defining trait is striving. It would be like painting a tiger without stripes to describe life in any other way. I had learned that the simplest death wasn't always the best after dealing with death for so long. We discussed it. Our families blessed us. We decided to become parents. We would continue to live rather than pass away.

With the drugs I was taking, assisted reproduction seemed to be my only option. So we went to a reproductive endocrinology clinic in Palo Alto to see a specialist. Although she was effective and professional, it was clear that she had little experience with patients who were terminally ill rather than infertile. With her eyes on her clipboard, she blasted through her pitch: "How long have you been trying?"

We haven't yet, though.

"Oh, I see. Naturally.

"Given your, uh, situation, I assume you want to get pregnant fast," she finally said.

"Yes," Lucy replied. "We want to get started immediately."

"Then, I would advise you to start with IVF," she said.

She appeared a little perplexed when I said that we'd prefer to reduce the number of embryos produced and destroyed. The majority of visitors valued expediency above all else. However, I was resolved to prevent the scenario in which Lucy found herself in charge of six embryos—the final pieces of our shared genomes, my final existence on this planet—stuck in a freezer somewhere, too painful to destroy, and impossible to fully humanize: technological artifacts that no one could relate to. We would need to produce at least a few embryos in vitro and implant the healthiest ones. After multiple intrauterine insemination trials, it became apparent that we needed a higher level of technology. The others would perish. Death had a role in this new life, even having children.

—

My first CT scan to assess Tarceva's effectiveness was scheduled for six weeks after I began treatment. I jumped out of the scanner, and the CT tech gave me a look. I'm not supposed to say this, Doc, but if you want to look at it, there's a computer back there. I entered my name as I loaded the pictures into the viewer.

The sign of acne was comforting. Although I was still constrained by exhaustion and back pain, my strength had also increased. As I sat there, I pondered what Emma had said. A tiny tumor growth would be a success if it was minimal. Naturally, my father had foreseen that the cancer would completely disappear. Using my family nickname, he had exclaimed, "Your scan will be clear, Pubby!" I took a deep breath, reminded myself that even a little growth was good, and clicked. Pictures appeared on the screen. Except for a one-centimeter nodule in the right upper lobe, my lungs, which had previously been speckled with countless tumors, were clear. I could see that my spine was starting to recover. The tumor burden had clearly and dramatically decreased.

I felt a wave of relief.

I had stable cancer.

Emma said, "You're well enough that we can meet every six weeks now," but she still wouldn't discuss the prognosis when we met her the following day. We can start discussing what your life might be like when we next get together. I sensed a new order settling in as the chaos of the previous months subsided. My tense sense of the future started to loosen up.

That weekend, there was a local gathering of Stanford neurosurgery alumni, and I eagerly anticipated the opportunity to reconnect with my former self. However, being there only made the bizarre contrast of my current life more apparent. Peers and seniors whose lives were on a different path than mine, whose bodies could still withstand standing for an exhausting eight-hour surgery, surrounded me with success, opportunity, and ambition. Victoria was opening the joyful gifts—grants, job offers, publications—that I should be sharing, and I felt like I was stuck in a reversed Christmas carol. The future my senior peers were living—early career awards, promotions, and new homes—was no longer mine.

I had no plans, so I was relieved that no one inquired about them. A paralyzing uncertainty hung over me even though I could now walk without a cane: Who would I be, moving forward, and for how long? Teacher, scientist, invalid? A bioethicist? Again, neurosurgeon, as Emma had suggested? Dad who stays at home? Author? Who am I, or should I be? I wanted to explore these moments with patients who had life-altering illnesses because, as a doctor, I had some understanding of what they faced. Therefore, wouldn't a terminal illness be the ideal present for the young man who had desired to comprehend death? Living it is the best way to comprehend it. However, I was unaware of how difficult it would be and how much land I would need to explore, map, and settle. I had always thought of the doctor's job as being like joining two sections of railroad track so that the patient could travel smoothly. The idea of confronting my own mortality was more disorienting and dislocating than I had anticipated. Looking into my own soul, I discovered that the fire was too weak and the tools too fragile to forge even my own conscience. I reflected on my younger self, who may have wanted to "forge in the smithy of my soul the uncreated conscience of my race."

I started reading literature again after becoming lost in the featureless wasteland of my own mortality and failing to find any direction in the endless curves of survival statistics, intracellular molecular pathways, and reams of scientific studies. These included: Tolstoy's Ivan Ilyich, B. S. Johnson's The Unfortunates, Woolf, Kafka, Montaigne, Frost, Greville, memoirs of cancer patients, and anything else written by anyone who had ever written about mortality. To start defining myself and moving forward once more, I was looking for a vocabulary that would help me understand death. I had strayed from literary and academic pursuits because of the luxury of firsthand experience, but now I felt compelled to reinterpret my own firsthand experiences to comprehend them. Hemingway used similar language to explain his method: gathering rich experiences, then withdrawing to reflect and write about them. I had to speak to continue.

I was therefore revived during this period by literature. Everywhere I looked, the shadow of death masked the significance of every action; the single-minded uncertainty of my future was killing me. I recall the moment when that seemingly insurmountable sea of uncertainty parted and my overwhelming uneasiness gave way. I awoke in agony and faced another day, with no project that seemed viable after breakfast. I thought, "I can't go on," and its antiphon instantly answered, adding the final seven words Samuel Beckett taught me as an undergraduate: "I'll go on." I climbed out of bed and walked forward, saying repeatedly, "I can't go on." I will continue.
I decided that morning that I would force myself to go back to the operating room. Why? since I was able to. Because I was that person. Because I would have to change the way I live from viewing death as an imposing, itinerant guest to understanding that, even though I am dying, I am still alive until I pass away.

———

I changed my physical therapy regimen over the course of the following six weeks, concentrating on developing strength for specific tasks like standing for extended periods of time, handling small objects with precision, and pronating to insert pedicle screws.

Then came another CT scan. The tumor had shrunk a bit. "I don't know how long you have, but I will say this: the patient I saw just before you today has been on Tarceva for seven years without any problems," Emma said as she went over the pictures with me. Before we feel that at ease with your cancer, you still have a ways to go. However, considering you, it is not absurd to consider living for ten years. It's not crazy, but you might not make it.

Prognosis--no,e justification—was right here. My rationale for going back to neurosurgery to revive myself. At the thought of ten years, a part of me rejoiced. "Returning to being a neurosurgeon is crazy for you—pick something easier," was something else that wished she had said. I was shocked to learn that despite everything, there had been one bright spot in the past few months: I didn't have to shoulder the enormous burden of the responsibilities required by neurosurgery. I also wanted to be released from having to shoulder the yoke once more. No one would have criticized me for not returning because neurosurgery is a very demanding field. (When someone asks me if it's a calling, I always say that it is. You cannot consider it a job because, if it were, it would be among the worst jobs in existence. "Shouldn't you be spending time with your family?" was a tactic used by a couple of my professors to actively discourage the idea. "Should you not?" I pondered. I was choosing to complete this task because it held sacred significance for me. Lucy and I had just arrived at the top of the hill. Below us were the famous buildings of Silicon Valley, each one named after a technological or biomedical advancement of the previous generation. But eventually, the desire to handle a surgical drill once more became too strong. The obligation to bear mortal responsibility drew me back into the operating room because moral obligation has weight and things with weight have gravity. Lucy was totally on board.

I informed the program director over the phone that I was prepared to go back. He was ecstatic. I discussed with Victoria the best way to reintroduce myself and catch up. In the event that something went wrong, I asked that a fellow resident always be there to support me. Also, I would only take on one case every day. I wouldn't be on call or supervise patients outside the operating room. We would take a cautious approach. When the operating room schedule was released, I was given a temporal lobectomy, which is one of my favorite procedures. Often, a misfiring hippocampal region deep within the temporal lobe is the cause of epilepsy. Epilepsy can be cured by removing the hippocampus, but this is a difficult procedure that involves carefully dissecting the hippocampus from the pia, the brain's delicate transparent covering, close to the brain stem.

I had spent the previous evening going over the anatomy and procedure steps in surgical textbooks. The angle of the head, the saw against the skull, and the way the light reflects off the pia after the temporal lobe is removed caused me to sleep restlessly. After getting out of bed, I dressed in a shirt and tie. (I assumed I would never need my scrubs again, so I returned them all months ago.) It had been eighteen weeks since I had arrived at the hospital and put on the familiar blue uniform. After checking with the patient to make sure there were no last-minute queries, I started organizing the operating room. The attending and I were cleaned up and prepared to start after the patient was intubated. I carefully cut the skin just above the ear with the scalpel, making sure I didn't forget anything and didn't make any mistakes. I used hooks to raise the skin flap after deepening the incision to the bone using electrocautery. It was all familiar, like muscle memory taking over. I drilled three holes in the skull with the drill. As I worked, the attendant sprayed water to keep the drill cool. I connected the holes using the craniotome, a sideways-cutting drill bit, which released a sizable chunk of bone. I cracked it with a crack. The silvery dura was lying there. Fortunately, I had avoided damaging it with the drill—a common mistake made by beginners. I opened the dura with a sharp knife so as not to damage the brain. Once more, success. I started to unwind. To keep the dura out of the way during the main surgery, I used tiny stitches to tack it back. The brain glistened and pulsed softly. The temporal lobe's top was adorned with immaculate Sylvian veins. The brain's well-known peach convolutions drew near.

The edges of my vision suddenly blurred. After setting down my instruments, I moved away from the table. A sensation of lightness overcame me as the blackness grew closer.

I apologized to the attending, saying, "I'm feeling a little faint, sir." I should probably lie down. My junior resident Jack will complete the case.

Jack showed up promptly, so I excused myself. I lay on the couch in the lounge and drank some orange juice. Twenty minutes later, I started to feel better. "Syncope due to neurocardiogenic causes," I muttered. The heart is momentarily stopped by the autonomic nervous system. Or a case of the nerves, as it is more widely referred to. An issue for a novice. I had not anticipated returning to the operating room in this manner. I went to the locker room, changed into my civilian clothes, and tossed my filthy scrubs in the laundry. As I was leaving, I picked up a pile of fresh scrubs. I promised myself tomorrow would be better.

Yes, it was. Each case seemed the same every day, but it proceeded a bit more slowly. I was extracting a degenerated disc from a patient's spine on the third day. I couldn't recall my precise move as I gazed at the protruding disc. My supervisor recommended using a rogue to take tiny bites.

"Yeah," I muttered, "I know that's the standard method, but there's another way.

For twenty minutes, I nibbled away, trying to think of the more refined method I had discovered for doing this. I quickly remembered it at the next spinal level.

I cried, "Cobb instrument!" "Kerrison, Mallet."

In thirty seconds, the entire disc was taken out. I replied, "That's how I do this."

My strength, fluency, and technique all continued to get better over the course of the following few weeks. My fingers recalled the old tricks they had once learned, and my hands were able to manipulate submillimeter blood vessels without getting hurt. A month later, I was running almost at capacity.

I only operated; Victoria and the other senior residents handled administration, patient care, and night and weekend calls. I needed to learn only the subtleties of complicated operations to feel complete because I had already mastered those skills. My days ended with me completely worn out, my muscles burning, and I was gradually getting better. In fact, it was devoid of joy. An iron focus on conquering the nausea, pain, and exhaustion had taken the place of the visceral pleasure I had once experienced from operating. Every night when I got home, I would eat a few painkillers and then crawl into bed beside Lucy, who had also resumed her full work schedule. The baby was due in June, when I would finish my residency, and she was now in the first trimester of her pregnancy. Just prior to implantation, a picture of our child as a blastocyst was taken. I said to Lucy, "She has your cell membrane.") Nevertheless, I was resolved to return my life to its previous course.

One more steady scan I resumed my job search six months after my diagnosis. I may have a few more years to live now that my cancer is under control. It appeared that the career I had spent years pursuing, which had vanished due to illness, was now within my grasp. I could practically hear a triumphal fanfare played by trumpets.

—

The next time I saw Emma, we discussed life and my current direction. I remembered Henry Adams attempting to draw a comparison between the existential force of the Virgin Mary and the scientific force of the combustion engine. Both were under the doctor's jurisdiction, but the existential questions were given more freedom now that the scientific ones had been resolved. I had recently been informed that, while I was away sick, the surgeon-scientist post at Stanford, for which I had been heir apparent, had been filled. I told her that I was devastated.

This doctor-professor relationship can be quite taxing, she admitted. However, you already know that. I apologize.

"Yeah, I suppose that the science that piqued my interest involved projects that would take twenty years. I'm not sure I'd be all that interested in becoming a scientist without that kind of time frame. I tried to comfort myself. "You can't accomplish much in a few years."

"All right. And never forget that you're doing fantastically. You're back to work. You are expecting a child. It's difficult for you to discover your values.

One of the younger professors, a close friend and former resident, stopped me in the hallway later that day.

She said, "Hey." "What to do with you has been a topic of much discussion in faculty meetings."

"How and what should I do?"

"I believe that some instructors are worried about your graduation."

I had already fulfilled a number of local and national requirements to graduate from residency, and I also needed the faculty's approval.

"What?" "I said." "I don't want to come across as arrogant, but I'm a competent surgeon, on par with—"

"I understand. They most likely just want to watch you carry out the duties of a chief, in my opinion. They like you, which is why. Really.

I came to see that it was accurate: I had only been functioning as a surgical technician for the last few months. I had been avoiding full responsibility for my patients by using cancer as an excuse. Still, damn, that was a good excuse. However, I began arriving earlier, staying later, and giving the patient's my whole attention once more, which added four hours to a twelve-hour day. It helped me always keep patients at the forefront of my thoughts. I battled waves of nausea, pain, and exhaustion during the first two days, thinking I would have to give up. In my downtime, I retreated to an unused bed to sleep. Even though my body was in ruins, I had started to enjoy it again by the third day. Reestablishing contact with patients restored the purpose of this work. Between cases and right before rounds, I took nonsteroidal anti-inflammatory drugs (NSAIDs) and antiemetics. I was in pain, but I was completely recovered. Rather than locating an unoccupied bed, I began to relax on the couch of the junior residents while I lectured and oversaw their patient care while experiencing a wave of back pain. I enjoyed doing the work more and more as my body became more and more tormented. I slept for forty hours straight at the end of the first week.

However, I was making the decisions: "Hey, boss," I said, "I was just going over the cases for tomorrow, and I believe it will be much safer and easier if we become parietal transcortical. I know the first case is scheduled interhemispheric."
"Really?" asked the attendant. "Allow me to view the movies. What do you know? You're correct. Is it possible to fix reservations?
The following day: "This is Paul. Hello, sir. I believe we'll have to take Mr. F for an ACDF tomorrow after seeing him and his family in the intensive care unit just now. Is it acceptable if I reserve it? What time do you have free time?

I quickly resumed my activities in the operating room: "Nurse, could you please page Dr. S? I intend to finish this case before he arrives.
"He's on the phone with me. "You can't possibly be done yet," he says. Breathless, the attending rushed in, cleaned up, and looked through the microscope.
I said, "I avoided the sinus by taking a slightly acute angle, but the entire tumor is gone."
"You managed to avoid the sinus?"
"Yes, sir."
"You managed to escape unscathed?"
"Yes, sir, you can look at it; it's on the table."

"It looks nice. Excellent. How did you become so quick? I apologize for not being here sooner.

"No issues."

The challenging aspect of illness is that it causes your values to shift over time. You make an effort to determine what is important to you, and you continue to do so. I had to learn how to budget because it felt like my credit card had been taken away. After two months, you might have a change of heart about your decision to become a neurosurgeon. After two months, you might want to focus on your church or learn how to play the saxophone. Living with a terminal illness is a process, though death is a one-time event.

I realized I had gone through the five stages of grief, the cliched "Denial → Anger → Bargaining → Depression → Acceptance," but I had done it in reverse. When I was diagnosed, I was dying. It had even made me feel good. I had agreed to it. I had been prepared. When it became apparent that I might not be dying so soon after all, I fell into a depression. This is obviously good news, but it's also perplexing and oddly draining. I might live another 12 months or 120 months because of the speed at which cancer science is developing and the nature of the statistics. The purpose of grand illnesses is to change people's lives. Rather, I was aware that I would die, but I had already known that. My knowledge level remained unchanged, but my ability to plan lunches had been severely damaged. If I knew how many months or years I had left, the path forward would seem clear. I would spend three months with my family. I would write a book if you told me one year. I'd return to treating illnesses in ten years. It didn't help that you have to live day by day: What should I do with that day?

So I started doing some negotiating, or rather, some negotiating. It would be more accurate to say: "God, I read Job, and I don't understand it, but if this is a test of faith, you now realize my faith is fairly weak, and my faith would have likely been tested if I hadn't left the spicy mustard off the pastrami sandwich. You know, you didn't have to go all out on me. Following the negotiation, angry outbursts followed: "I've worked my entire life to reach this point, and then you give me cancer?"

And perhaps, at last, I had reached denial. Complete denial, perhaps. Perhaps we should just assume that we will live a long life since we have no other certainty. That might be the only option.

—

My diagnosis was nine months ago, and I was working until late at night or early in the morning, focused on graduating. My physical condition was deteriorating. When I got home, I was too exhausted to eat. I had been gradually increasing the dosage of NSAIDs, antiemetics, and Tylenol. I had a chronic cough that was probably brought on by the dead tumor's scarring in my lungs. I reminded myself that I only needed to maintain this unrelenting pace for a few more months before I would graduate from residency and transition into the relatively more relaxed position of a professor.

I took a plane to Wisconsin for a job interview in February. A tenure-track professorship, millions of dollars to launch a neuroscience lab, leadership of my own clinical service, flexibility if I needed it for my health, attractive job options for Lucy, a high salary, gorgeous scenery, an idyllic town, and the ideal boss were all on offer. The department chairman informed me, "I understand your health, and you probably have a strong connection with your oncologist." We can fly you back and forth if you would like to continue receiving care there, but if you would like to look into it, we do have a first-rate cancer center here. Is there anything more I can do to increase the appeal of this position?

I considered what Emma had said. With the force of a religious conversion, I had changed from not believing I could be a surgeon to actually being one. Even when I couldn't remember it, she had always remembered this aspect of who I was. She had accomplished what I had pushed myself to do years before as a physician. She had taken mortal responsibility for my soul and brought me back to a place where I could find myself again. I had reached the pinnacle of neurosurgical training, poised to become a surgeon-scientist and a neurosurgeon. Every trainee strives for this objective, but very few succeed.

After dinner that evening, the chairman was driving me back to my hotel. He pulled over and stopped the vehicle. He said, "Let me show you something." We exited and stood before the hospital, overlooking a frozen lake with flecks of light leaking from faculty houses along its far edge. You can sail or swim to work in the summer. You can ice-skate or ski in the winter.

It resembled a dream. I suddenly realised it was a fantasy. We were never able to relocate to Wisconsin. What if, after two years, I experienced a significant relapse? Lucy would be alone, without family or friends, and responsible for a new baby and a dying husband. I recognized that the calculus had been altered by cancer, despite my best efforts to avoid it. I had spent the last few months doing everything in my power to return my life to its pre-cancer course and prevent cancer from taking any more of my life. As much as I wanted to feel victorious now, I felt like I was being held back by the crab's claws. My life was made strange and tense by the curse of cancer, which made it difficult for me to be neither blind to nor constrained by the imminence of death. Long shadows were cast even when the cancer was in retreat.

I had comforted myself with the notion that managing a lab only made sense over a twenty-year period when I had initially lost my professorship at Stanford. I realized now that this was indeed the case. Freud was a successful neuroscientist early in his career. He put down his microscope when he realized that neuroscience would not be able to match his genuine goal of comprehending the mind for at least a century. I believe I had a similar feeling. My diagnosis had prolonged the odds of my research endeavors to transform neurosurgery, so I didn't want to spend the rest of my money in a lab.

Emma's voice came back to me: You need to determine what matters most to you.

What would I have wanted if I didn't want to be the best neurosurgeon and neuroscientist?

To become a dad?

To work as a neurosurgeon?

To instruct?

I had no idea. Even though I was unsure of what I wanted, I had learned something that Hippocrates, Maimonides, and Osler had not: a doctor's job is not to prevent death or restore patients to their former lives, but to take a patient and their family into our arms and care for them until they are able to stand again, face their own existence, and make sense of it.

My own conceit as a surgeon now exposed me. Despite my intense focus on my role and influence over patients' lives, these were, at most, transient roles and powers. The patient and family continue to live their lives after an acute crisis has been handled, the patient has been awakened, extubated, and released, but nothing is ever quite the same. The words of a doctor can calm the mind, just as a neurosurgeon's scalpel can calm a brain ailment. However, there is still work to be done to address their emotional and physical morbidities and uncertainties.

Emma had not restored my previous identity. She had safeguarded my capacity to create a new one. Finally, I realized that I would have to.

———

My parents flew in from Arizona for a weekend visit, and Lucy and I attended church on a crystal-clear spring morning on the third Sunday of Lent. My mother engaged the family seated next to us in conversation as we sat in a long wooden pew. She began by praising the mother's baby daughter's eyes before swiftly switching to more serious topics, demonstrating her abilities as a connector, confidante, and listener. I started laughing out loud during the pastor's Bible reading. Jesus was depicted as frustrated, and his followers took his metaphorical language literally:

"Everyone who drinks this water will experience thirst again, but whoever drinks the water I shall give will never experience thirst; the water I shall give will become in him a spring of water welling up to eternal life," Jesus replied in response to her question. "Sir, please give me this water so that I won't be thirsty or have to come here to get water all the time," the woman said to him.

… "Rabbi, eat," the disciples begged him in the meantime. However, he told them, "I have food to eat that you are unaware of." "Could someone have brought him something to eat?" the disciples asked each other.

After attending college, when my understanding of God and Jesus had become, to put it mildly, shaky, it was passages like these, which clearly mock literalist interpretations of Scripture, that had led me back to Christianity. The main weapon used against Christianity during my time as an ironclad atheist had been its empirical failure. Enlightened reason must have provided a more logical universe. Undoubtedly, the faithful were liberated from blind faith by Occam's razor. It is irrational to believe in God since there is no evidence for him.

I, like most scientific types, came to believe in the possibility of a material conception of reality, an ultimately scientific worldview that would grant a complete metaphysics, minus outdated concepts like souls, God, and bearded white men in robes, despite having grown up in a devout Christian home where prayer and Scripture readings were a nightly ritual. Building a framework for such an undertaking took up a significant portion of my twenties. However, the issue eventually became clear. To make science the arbiter of metaphysics is to exclude not only God but also love, hate, and meaning—to think of a world that is obviously different from the one we live in. This is not to imply that you have to believe in God if you think that life has purpose. To put it another way, if you think that science doesn't support God, you're practically forced to conclude that it doesn't support meaning, which means that life itself doesn't either. In other words, all knowledge is scientific knowledge, and existential claims are meaningless.

The problem is that since scientific methodology is the result of human labor, it is unable to arrive at a definitive truth. We construct scientific theories to categorize and control the world and break down phenomena into digestible chunks. Reproducibility and artificial objectivity are the cornerstones of science. This makes scientific knowledge inapplicable to the existential, visceral nature of human life, which is distinct, subjective, and unpredictable, even though it makes it powerful enough to produce claims about matter and energy. The ability of science to organize empirical, reproducible data may be the most helpful method, but it is based on its incapacity to understand the most fundamental elements of human existence, such as hope, fear, love, hate, beauty, envy, honor, weakness, striving, suffering, and virtue.

There will always be a disconnect between scientific theory and these fundamental interests. The entire human experience cannot be captured by any one system of thought. After all, Occam maintained that revelation, not atheism, is still the domain of metaphysics. And these are the only grounds on which atheism can be justified. Therefore, Graham Greene's commandant from The Power and the Glory is the quintessential atheist, whose atheism stems from a revelation of God's absence. Only a world-making vision can be the foundation of true atheism. Many atheists' favorite quote, "The ancient covenant is in pieces; man at last knows that he is alone in the unfeeling immensity of the universe, out of which he emerged only by chance," from French biologist Jacques Monod, the winner of the Nobel Prize, obscures this revelatory aspect.

Yet I returned to the central values of Christianity—sacrifice, redemption, forgiveness—because I found them so compelling. There is a tension in the Bible between justice and mercy, between the Old Testament and the New Testament. Furthermore, according to the New Testament, goodness is the standard, and you can never measure up to it. Jesus' central message, in my opinion, is that mercy always triumphs over justice.

Furthermore, it's possible that the fundamental lesson of original sin isn't "feel guilty all the time." Perhaps it is more like this: "Everyone has an idea of what it means to be good, and we can't always live up to it." Maybe that's what the New Testament message is, after all. You cannot live that way, even if your idea is as clear-cut as Leviticus. It's crazy, not just impossible.

I couldn't say anything definitive about God, of course, but the fundamental facts of human existence strongly contradict naive determinism. Furthermore, nobody—including myself—ascribes any epistemic authority to revelation. We are all rational beings; revelation is insufficient. We would dismiss it as delusional even if God spoke to us.

What is the would-be metaphysician to do, I wonder?

Give up?

Nearly.

Aim for the capital-T Truth, but acknowledge that it is impossible to accomplish—or that even if a right answer is possible, verification is undoubtedly impossible.

Ultimately, it is undeniable that we can only see a portion of the picture. First the physician, then the patient, then the engineer, then the economist, then the pearl diver, the alcoholic, the cable guy, the sheep farmer, the Indian beggar, the pastor, and finally the doctor. One person can never possess all of human knowledge. It develops from the connections we make with the outside world and with each other, but it is never fully realized. And above all of them, as at the conclusion of that Sunday's reading, Truth comes.

Together, the reaper and the sower can celebrate. The adage "One sows and another reaps" is validated here. Others have done the work, and you are enjoying the results of their labor; I sent you to reap what you have not worked for.

———

Seven months after my return to surgery, I jumped out of the CT scanner. This would be my final scan prior to completing my residency, becoming a father, and the actualization of my future.
"Do you want to have a look, Doc?" the technician asked.
"Not at this time," I replied. "Today is going to be a very busy day for me."
Six o'clock had arrived. In addition to scheduling tomorrow's OR, I had to go see patients, review movies, dictate my clinic notes, check on my post-op, and more. I took a seat next to a radiology viewing station in the neurosurgery office at about eight o'clock in the evening. I switched it on, checked the scans of my two easy spine cases for the following day, and then entered my name. I flipped through the pictures like a child flipping through a flip book, contrasting the most recent scan with the previous one. Everything had the same appearance, and the old tumors were still there. Wait, except.

I reverted the pictures. looked once more.
It was there. My right middle lobe is filled with a new, large tumor. Strangely, it appeared as though a full moon had nearly risen above the horizon. Returning to the old pictures, I could see the smallest hint of it, a spectral forerunner now fully realized.
I wasn't scared or angry. It just was. Like the distance between the sun and the earth, it was a fact about the world. I told Lucy as I drove home. Lucy and I sat down in the living room with our laptops and laid out the next course of action: biopsies, tests, and chemotherapy. It was a Thursday night, and we wouldn't see Emma again until

Monday. This time, the chances of a long life would be slimmer, and the treatments would be harder to endure. Eliot once again: "But I hear the rattle of the bones at my back in a cold blast, and a laugh that spreads from ear to ear." For weeks, months, or even forever, neurosurgery would not be feasible. However, we agreed that all this could wait until Monday to actually happen. It was Thursday, and I had already prepared the OR assignments for tomorrow. I intended to spend my final day as a resident.

I took a deep breath as I got out of my car at the hospital at five twenty the following morning, smelling the eucalyptus and—was that pine? I hadn't previously noticed that. When the resident team got together for morning rounds, I got to meet them. The morbidity and mortality conference, or M&M, is a regular meeting where neurosurgeons gather to discuss mistakes made and cases that have gone wrong. After reviewing overnight events, new admissions, and new scans, we went to see our patients. After that, I spoke with a patient, Mr. R, for a few minutes. After I removed his brain tumor, he developed a rare syndrome known as Gerstmann's, in which he started exhibiting a number of specific deficits, including the inability to write, name fingers, perform arithmetic, and distinguish left from right. Eight years ago, when I was a medical student, I witnessed it for the first time on one of the first patients I followed on the neurosurgical service. Mr. R shared his euphoria, and I pondered whether that was a feature of the syndrome that had never been previously described. However, Mr. R was improving: his arithmetic was only marginally off, and his speech had nearly returned to normal. He would probably fully recover.

I scrubbed for my final case after the morning was over. The moment suddenly felt huge. When did I last scrub? This might have been it. I watched as the suds trickled down the drain and off my arms. Making sure the corners were clean and sharp, I draped the patient, gowned up, and went into the operating room. This case had to be flawless. I made his lower back's skin open. He was an old man with degenerated spine that caused excruciating pain by compressing his nerve roots. I felt the tips of his vertebrae as I pushed away the fat until the fascia showed. I carefully separated the muscle by opening the fascia, until only the broad, shiny vertebrae—bloodless and clean—were visible through the incision. As I started to remove the lamina, the back wall of the vertebrae, whose bony overgrowths and ligaments underneath were compressing the nerves, the attending wandered in.

"Looks nice," he remarked. "I can have the guy come in and finish if you want to attend the conference today."

I was starting to feel pain in my back. Why hadn't I taken an additional NSAID dose in advance? However, this case should be resolved quickly. I was nearly there.

"No," I replied. "I want the case to be resolved."

Together, we finished the bony removal after the attending scrubbed in. He started tearing at the ligaments, which were covered by the dura, which held the nerve roots and spinal fluid. At this point, tearing a hole in the dura is the most frequent mistake. Meanwhile, I worked. I noticed a flash of blue—the dura beginning to show through—near his instrument out of the corner of my eye.

"Be careful!" As his instrument's mouth sank into the dura, I spoke. The wound started to fill with clear spinal fluid. It had been over a year since I had a leak in one of my cases. Repairs would take another hour. I said, "Get the micro set out." "There is a leak."

My shoulders were burned by the time the repair was complete and the compressive soft tissue was taken out. I was left to close after the attendant apologized, thanked me, and broke scrub. The layers fit together well. I started using a running nylon stitch to suture the skin. Although most surgeons used staples, I was certain that nylon had a lower rate of infection, so we would do this last closure the way I wanted. As though there had been no surgery at all, the skin came together flawlessly and without any tension.

Excellent. One positive thing.

"You on call this weekend, Doc?" asked the scrub nurse, who I had never worked with before, as we untangled the patient.

"Nope." And perhaps never again.

"Do you have any more cases today?

"Nope." And perhaps never again.

"Well, I suppose that means there will be a happy ending! The work is finished. Doc, I prefer happy endings, don't you?

Indeed. Indeed, I enjoy happy endings.

While the anesthesiologists started to wake the patient and the nurses cleaned, I sat down by the computer to enter orders. I had always joked that when I was in charge, we would only listen to bossa nova in the OR rather than the upbeat pop tunes that everyone enjoyed. The gentle, melodic sounds of a saxophone filled the room as I turned on Getz/Gilberto on the radio.

Shortly after, I left the operating room and collected my belongings, which had accumulated over seven years of work: toothbrushes, bars of soap, phone chargers, snacks, my skull model, my collection of neurosurgery books, extra sets of clothes for the nights you don't leave, and so forth. I later realised I had forgotten my books. Here, they would be more useful.

A man came up to ask me a question on my way to the parking lot, but his pager went off. "I'll catch you later!" he called over his shoulder as he glanced at it, waved, and dashed back into the hospital. I sat in the car, turned the key, and slowly pulled into the street crying. I pulled into my house, hung up my white coat, removed my ID badge, and walked through the front door. I took my pager's battery out. After removing my scrubs, I had a lengthy shower.

I called Victoria later that evening to inform her that I would not be setting the OR schedule and would not be in on Monday, if at all.

She remarked, "You know, I've been having this recurring nightmare that this day is approaching." "How you managed to do this for so long is beyond me."

103

On Monday, Lucy and I met Emma. The plan we had envisioned—bronchoscopic biopsy, search for targetable mutations, otherwise chemotherapy—was confirmed by her. However, my true purpose for being there was to assist her. I informed her of my leave from neurosurgery.

"All right," she said. That's alright. If, for example, you would like to concentrate on something more important to you, you can stop neurosurgery. Not because you are sick. You haven't gotten any sicker in the past week. Although this is a setback, you can continue on your current course. For you, neurosurgery was crucial.

I had crossed the boundaries from subject to direct object, from actor to acted upon, and from doctor to patient once more. One could think of my life before becoming ill as the linear sum of my decisions. His and other people's actions determined a character's destiny, just like in the majority of contemporary stories. Gloucester in King Lear may lament human fate as "flies to wanton boys," but the play's dramatic arc is initiated by Lear's conceit. The individual took center stage after the Enlightenment. However, I now lived in a different, older world that was more Greek tragedy than Shakespeare, where human deeds were insignificant in comparison to superhuman forces. Oedipus and his parents are powerless to change their fates. The only way they can gain insight into the forces governing their lives is via oracles and seers, who possess divine vision. The solace of oracular wisdom was what I had come for, not a treatment plan—I had read enough to understand the medical paths forward.

She must have said, "This is not the end," a thousand times—did I not give similar speeches to my own patients?—to those who were looking for unattainable answers. Or perhaps the start of the end. The beginning is just getting started.

I also felt better.

The nurse practitioner, Alexis, called a week following the biopsy. Chemotherapy was the only treatment available because there were no new targetable mutations, and it was scheduled for Monday. When I inquired about the specific agents, I was informed that I would need to speak with Emma. She would call me over the weekend, but she was on her way to Lake Tahoe with her children.

Emma called Saturday the next day. I wanted to know her opinion on chemotherapy drugs.

"All right," she said. "Are you thinking of anything in particular?"

"I suppose the primary inquiry is whether or not to incorporate Avastin," I remarked. I am aware that some cancer centers are rejecting it because of the conflicting data and the additional possible negative effects. However, given the large number of studies that support its use, I would lean toward including it. If I have a negative reaction, we can stop using it. if you think it makes sense.

Yes, that seems about correct. Another reason to use it up front is that insurance companies make it difficult to add it later.

"I appreciate you calling. I'll let you resume your enjoyment of the lake.

"All right. However, there is one thing. She hesitated. "Obviously, you're a doctor, you know what you're talking about, and it's your life, so I'm really happy that we can work together to create your medical plan. However, I'm also happy to simply act as the doctor if that's what you want at any point.

I never thought I could absolve myself of the duty to take care of my own health. I had simply assumed that every patient became an expert in their own condition. I recalled how, as a naive green medical student, I would frequently wind up asking patients to describe their conditions and therapies to me, including their pink pills and blue toes. However, as a physician, I always assumed responsibility for my patients and never expected them to make decisions on their own. And I came to the realization that I was attempting to accomplish the same thing now, with my patient-self still being accountable to my doctor-self. Perhaps a Greek god had cursed me, but it seemed reckless, if not impossible, to give up control.

—

On Monday, chemotherapy started. My mother, Lucy, and I visited the infusion facility together. I sat down in an easy chair, had an IV inserted, and waited. The drug cocktail infusion would take four and a half hours. With Lucy and my mother beside me, breaking the quiet with sporadic small talk, I spent the time napping, reading, and occasionally just staring. The other people in the room were in different states of health: some were dapper, some were bald, some were well-groomed, some were withered, some were lively, and some were unkempt. With IV tubing dripping poison into outstretched arms, everyone lay motionless and silent. I was supposed to go back for treatment every three weeks.

The following day, I started to feel the effects, a severe bone-weariness and a deep fatigue. Eating was like drinking seawater, which is normally a very pleasant experience. All my pleasures were suddenly tainted. Lucy made me a bagel with cream cheese for breakfast, and it was salty and delicious. I put it down. It was draining to read. I had consented to contribute a few chapters to two important neurosurgical textbooks about the therapeutic potential of my research with V. I put that aside as well. Time was marked by forced feedings and television as the days passed. Over the course of the weeks, a pattern emerged: the malaise would gradually subside, and normalcy would return in time for the subsequent treatment.

The cycles went on; I kept going in and out of the hospital with minor issues that prevented me from going back to work. After determining that I had fulfilled all local and national requirements for graduation, the neurosurgery department set the ceremony for a Saturday, roughly two weeks prior to Lucy's due date.

The day came. I felt a sharp nausea as I stood in our bedroom getting ready for graduation, which was the end of seven years of residency. This was not like the typical chemotherapy nausea, which came on like a wave and could be ridden. I started throwing up green bile, which had a chalky flavor that was different from stomach acid. This came straight from my stomach.

After all, I wouldn't be attending graduation.

Lucy drove me to the emergency room, where rehydration started because I needed IV fluids to prevent dehydration. The diarrhea replaced the vomiting. In our friendly conversation, Brad, the medical resident, and I reviewed my medical history and all my prescriptions. We then talked about the latest developments in molecular therapies, particularly Tarceva, which I was still taking. The medical plan was straightforward: until I was able to consume enough fluids orally, I would be kept hydrated with intravenous fluids. I was admitted to a hospital room that night. However, I discovered Tarceva was missing from my medication list when the nurse went over it. To rectify the mistake, I asked her to call the resident. These things do occur. After all, I was on a dozen prescriptions. It was difficult to stay on track.

Brad showed up well after midnight.

He inquired, "I heard you had a question about your medications."

"Yes," I replied. "Tarceva was not ordered." Would you mind placing the order?

"I chose to remove you from it."

"Why is that?"

"You cannot handle it because your liver enzymes are too high."

I couldn't understand. Why hadn't we talked about it earlier if my elevated liver enzymes for months were a problem? This was obviously a mistake, anyway. "Your boss, Emma, my oncologist, has seen these figures and wants to keep me updated."

Medical decisions must frequently be made by residents without consulting the attending physician. But he would undoubtedly give in now that he knew Emma's viewpoint.

"But it may be contributing to your gastrointestinal issues."

My perplexity grew. The conversation usually ends when the attending orders are invoked. I said, "I haven't had any issues taking it for a year." "You believe that Tarceva, rather than the chemotherapy, is the cause of this now?"

"Well, maybe."

Anger took the place of confusion. Was this young person, barely older than my junior residents and two years out of medical school, really arguing with me? If he were correct, that would be one thing, but he was illogical. Did I not mention this afternoon that my bone metastases become active and cause excruciating pain if I don't take that pill? I don't want to come across as dramatic, but this hurts much more than breaking bones while boxing. In other words, excruciating pain. In other words, I'll be screaming in pain soon.

"Well, considering the drug's half-life, that probably won't happen for a day or so."

I could see that Brad saw me as a problem, a box to be checked, rather than a patient.

We wouldn't even be having this conversation if you weren't you, he went on. I'd just cut off the drug and force you to demonstrate that it's the source of your suffering.

What had become of our friendly conversation this afternoon? When I was in medical school, I recalled a patient who told me she always wore her most expensive socks to the doctor's office. This way, the doctor would see that she was a serious person who should be treated with respect when she was in a patient's gown and without shoes. (Well, there's the issue—I had been stealing hospital socks for years, and I was wearing them!)

In any case, Tarceva is a unique medication that needs to be approved by a fellow or attending. For this, do you really want me to wake someone up? Why not wait until morning?

And there it was.

He had to make an embarrassing phone call with his boss to admit his mistake to fulfill his duty to me. He was a night shift worker. The majority of programs were compelled to implement shift work due to residency education regulations. Additionally, shift work entails a

To controlling hands
I leaned back in my hospital bed and closed my eyes. As the darkness of delirium descended again, I finally relaxed.

—

After Lucy's due date passed without any labor, I was eventually set to leave the hospital. Since my diagnosis, I have shed more than forty pounds, with fifteen of those pounds coming in the last week. Although my hair had significantly thinned since then, primarily in the last month, I still weighed the same as I had in eighth grade. I was awake once more, aware of the outside world, but I had wilted. My bones were a living X-ray, visible against my skin. It was exhausting just to hold my head at home. It took two hands to lift a glass of water. It was impossible to read.

To assist, both parents were in town. Lucy experienced her first contractions two days after being discharged. While my mother drove me to my follow-up appointment with Emma, she stayed home.
"Angry?" Emma inquired.
"No."
"You ought to be. It will take time to recover.
"Well, all right. In the grand scheme of things, I am frustrated. On a daily basis, however, I'm prepared to resume physical therapy and begin my recuperation. It should be old hat since I've already done it once.
She inquired, "Did you see your last scan?"
"No, I've sort of given up looking."
"It appears to be good," she said. "The illness appears to be stable, possibly even reducing slightly."
We discussed some upcoming logistics. Until I recovered, chemotherapy would be put on hold. I also wouldn't be accepted in my current state for experimental trials. I had to get stronger before I could get treatment. I supported my neck's faltering muscles by leaning my head against the wall. My mind was confused. I needed that oracle to

scry once more, to extract secrets from Kaplan-Meier graphs or mutant genes, from star charts or birds.

I asked, "What's the next step, Emma?"
"Be more resilient. That's all.
However, when the cancer returns... The probabilities, that is. I stopped. Tarceva, the first-line treatment, had not worked. Chemotherapy, or second-line therapy, had almost killed me. Third-line therapy promised little, if I could get there at all. The vast unknown of experimental treatments comes next. Doubtful words escaped my lips. "Returning to the operating room, walking, or even—"
She said, "You have five good years left."
She said it without the assurance of a sincere believer and without the commanding voice of an oracle. Instead, she uttered it as a request. similar to that patient who could only communicate numerically. Like a mere human, with whatever forces and fates actually control these things, she was pleading with me more than she was speaking. We were a doctor and a patient in a relationship that, at times, like right now, had a magisterial quality. But other times, it was just two people huddled together, one facing the abyss.

It turns out that doctors also require hope.
Lucy's mother called to inform her that they were going to the hospital while they were on their way home from the appointment with Emma. Lucy was giving birth. I advised her to inquire about the epidural as soon as possible. She had endured enough pain.) My father pushed me in a wheelchair back to the hospital. In the delivery room, I lay on a cot with blankets and heat packs to prevent my skeletal body from shivering. I watched Lucy and the nurse go through the labor ritual for the next two hours. The nurse counted off the pushing as a contraction intensified, saying, "And a one two three four five six seven eight nine and a ten!"

Lucy smiled as she turned to face me. She remarked, "I feel like I'm participating in a sport."

As I watched her belly grow, I grinned back while lying on the cot. Lucy's and my daughter's lives would be filled with so many absences; if this was the only way I could be present, then so be it.

The nurse jolted me awake sometime after midnight. "Time is almost here," she muttered. After gathering the blankets, she assisted me in finding a chair beside Lucy. The obstetrician, who was no older than I, was already present in the room. When the baby was crowning, she glanced up at me. She remarked, "I can tell you one thing: your daughter has hair just like yours." "And lots of it." As Lucy was nearing the end of her labor, I nodded and held her hand. Then, with a last push, she appeared on July 4 at 2:11 a.m. We had chosen Elizabeth Acadia—Cady months earlier.

The nurse asked me if we could put her on your skin, Papa.

With my teeth chattering, I said, "No, I'm too c-c-cold." "However, I wish I could hold her."

They gave her to me after wrapping her in blankets. The possibilities of life radiated before us as we felt her weight in one arm and held Lucy's hand in the other. My body's cancer cells would either continue to die or begin to proliferate once more. Rather than seeing a desolate wasteland, I saw something more straightforward: a blank page that I would continue on.

—

However, our home is dynamic.

Cady develops day by day, week by week: a first laugh, a first smile, a first grasp. Her pediatrician on charts routinely documents her growth, with tick marks signifying her advancement over time. A dazzling freshness envelops her. An incandescence illuminates the room as she smiles while sitting in my lap, mesmerized by my tuneless singing.

I now view time as having two sides. Each day moves me closer to the next relapse and, ultimately, death, while also pulling me further away from the low point of my most recent relapse. Maybe later than I want, but definitely sooner than I want. I imagine there are two reactions to that insight. Perhaps the most evident is a desire for frantic activity: to "live life to the fullest," to travel, to eat, to fulfill a variety of unfulfilled goals. Cancer is cruel in part because it not only takes up your time but also depletes your energy, making it much harder to get as much done in a day. A weary hare is now racing. And I'd rather take a more tortoise-like approach, even if I had the energy. I think, I plod. Some days I just keep going.

Does time contract when one moves hardly at all, if it dilates when one moves at high speeds? Days are much shorter, so it must be.
Time has started to feel stagnant, with little to differentiate one day from the next. "The time is two forty-five" and "I'm going through a tough time" are two different ways that we use the word "time" in English. These days, time seems more like a state of being than a ticking clock. Language becomes comfortable. A sense of openness prevails. The clock's hands may have seemed arbitrary to me as a surgeon in the operating room, but I never considered them to be meaningless. The day of the week is hardly more significant now than the time of day. Medical school is a relentlessly forward-looking program that emphasizes delayed gratification; you're constantly considering your career goals five years from now. However, I have no idea what I will be doing in five years. I might not be alive. Maybe I'm not. I might be in good health. Maybe I'm writing. I'm not sure. Therefore, thinking about the future—that is, after lunch—is not really helpful.
Additionally, verb conjugation has become confused. Which statement—"I am a neurosurgeon," "I was a neurosurgeon," or "I was and will be a neurosurgeon again"—is true? According to Graham Greene, the first twenty years of life are spent living, and the rest is spent reflecting. What tense do I currently inhabit? Have I moved into the past perfect tense from the present tense? On the lips of others, the future tense appears blank and startling. It seemed impolite to reply,

"Well...probably not," when old friends called out parting vows, such as, "We'll see you at the twenty-fifth!" A few months ago, I celebrated my fifteenth college reunion at Stanford by standing out on the quad, sipping whiskey as a pink sun dipped below the horizon.

Everybody falls victim to finitude. I have a feeling that I'm not the only person achieving this perfect condition. Most aspirations are fulfilled or shelved. Either way, they are history. The future flattens out into an endless present rather than serving as a ladder toward life's objectives. Money, status, and all the other vanity that the Ecclesiastes preacher described are of little interest; they are, in fact, chasing after the wind.

However, one thing—our daughter Cady—cannot be deprived of her future. I'm hoping I'll be around long enough for her to remember me. Words last longer than I do. What would they say? I had considered leaving her a string of letters. I have no idea what this girl will be like when she turns fifteen, or even whether she will accept the moniker we have given her. To this baby, who is all future, who briefly overlaps with me, whose life is, barring the unlikely, all but past, there may be only one thing to say.

The message is straightforward: I pray that you do not discount the fact that you filled a dying man's days with a sated joy—a joy that I had never experienced in all of my previous years, a joy that does not hunger for more and more but rests, satisfied—when you reach one of the many times in life when you must give an account of yourself, a ledger of what you have been, done, and meant to the world. At this moment, that is a huge situation.

EPILOGUE

Lucy Kalanithi

You left me, sweet, two legacies,—
A legacy of love
A Heavenly Father would content,
Had he the offer of;
You left me boundaries of pain
Capacious as the sea,
Between eternity and time,
Your consciousness and me.

—Emily Dickinson

His mother grinned and exclaimed, "I really like him."

We hoped the peaceful weekend would continue Sunday. We would go to church and then take Cady and her cousin to the baby swings at the park up the hill if Paul felt well enough. We would share our grief, continue to process the recent upsetting news, and cherish our time together.

Instead, time accelerated.

Paul had a fever of 104 degrees when I stroked his forehead early on Sunday morning, but he was otherwise quite comfortable and showed no new symptoms. After starting antibiotics in case of pneumonia (Paul's chest X-ray was dense with tumors, which could obscure an infection), Paul's father and Suman joined us as we left the emergency room in a matter of hours and headed home to be with the rest of the family. Instead, though, was the cancer spreading quickly? Paul was very sick, but he slept well that afternoon. As I watched him sleep, I began to cry. I then slipped into our living room and his father's tears joined mine. I've already missed him.

On Sunday night, Paul's health suddenly deteriorated. In a shocking shift, he sat on the edge of our bed, gasping for air. I made an ambulance call. "This might be how it ends," Paul said to me in a whisper as we reentered the emergency room, him on a gurney this time, his parents right behind us.

I said, "I'm with you here."

As usual, Paul received a warm welcome from the hospital staff. But as soon as they saw his condition, they took swift action. Following preliminary testing, they covered his mouth and nose with a mask to aid in his breathing using BiPAP, a breathing support device that performed a large portion of his breathing for him by supplying a powerful, mechanical flow of air each time he inhaled. Even though BiPAP aids in respiratory mechanics, it can be difficult for patients because it is loud and forceful, causing their lips to split apart with each breath like a dog's head out a car window. As the steady whoosh, whoosh of the machine started, I stood close, leaning over the gurney, and put my hand in Paul's.

Paul's blood carbon dioxide level was extremely high, a sign that his breathing effort was becoming too much for him. According to blood tests, his lung disease and debility had progressed over days to weeks, causing some of the excess carbon dioxide to build up. He was still lucid because his brain had gradually adjusted to higher-than-normal carbon dioxide levels. He watched. As a doctor, he recognized alarming test results. As he was wheeled to an intensive-care unit, where a large number of his own patients had suffered either before or after neurosurgery, with their families gathered in vinyl chairs by their bedsides, I could relate to them as well. When we got there, he asked me in between BiPAP breaths, "Will I need to be intubated?" "Do I need to be intubated?"

Paul talked about that issue all night long with his doctors, with his family, and then with me alone. Paul's longtime mentor, the critical-care attendant, arrived at midnight to talk with the family about treatment options. He argued BiPAP was only a short-term fix. Paul would need to be intubated, or placed on a ventilator, as the only other option. Was he looking for that?

The crucial query soon emerged: Is it possible to reverse the abrupt respiratory failure?

There was concern Paul might not recover enough to ever leave the ventilator. Would he be lost to delirium and then organ failure, his body and mind slipping away one after the other? As doctors, we had seen this painful situation. Paul considered the alternative: he could opt for "comfort care" instead of intubation, but death would arrive sooner and with greater certainty. Considering brain cancer, he remarked, "Even if I survive this, I'm not sure I see a future that includes meaningful time." Desperately, his mother added. She said, "No decisions tonight, Pubby." "We should all get some sleep." Paul consented after confirming his "do not resuscitate" status. Sympathetic nurses brought him extra blankets. I turned the fluorescent lights off.

Paul was able to sleep until dawn, his father keeping watch while I took a quick nap in a nearby room to maintain my mental fortitude, knowing that the next day might be the most difficult of my life. At six in the morning, with the lights still low and the intensive-care monitors chiming sporadically, I slipped back into Paul's room. Paul's eyes opened. We discussed "comfort care" once more, avoiding drastic measures to stop his decline, and he asked out loud if he could return home. I was concerned that he might suffer and pass away en route because he was so sick. But I nodded that yes, comfort care might be the way we were going, and I promised to do everything in my power to get him home if that was what he valued most. Or could home be recreated here in some way? Between puffs of BiPAP, he replied: "Cady."

Unaffected by the BiPAP machine as it continued to blow, keeping Paul alive, Cady arrived quickly—our friend Victoria had picked her up from her house—and started her own unintentional, joyful vigil while contentedly nestled in the crook of Paul's right arm, batting at his hospital blankets, smiling, and cooing.

Outside the room, Paul's family and I joined the medical team as they made rounds and talked about Paul's condition. Paul's acute respiratory failure was probably caused by rapidly spreading cancer. His carbon dioxide level continued to rise, which is a solid sign that he should be intubated. The family was divided because Paul's oncologist had called in the hopes that the urgent issue could be resolved, but the on-site doctors were less hopeful. I implored them to consider reversing his sudden decline as strongly as possible.

I said, "He doesn't want a Hail Mary." "He wants to remove the mask and hold Cady if he doesn't have a chance of meaningful time."
I went back to Paul's bed. "I'm ready," he said clearly in a soft but firm voice as he glanced at me with his dark eyes alert above the BiPAP mask's nose bridge.
He meant that he was prepared to stop breathing support, start taking morphine, and pass away.
The family got together. We all showed our love and respect for Paul in the brief minutes following his decision. Paul's eyes gleamed with tears. He was appreciative of his parents. He requested that we see to it that his manuscript was published in some way. He expressed his love for me one final time. "Paul, your family will fall apart after you die, but they'll pull it back together because of the example of bravery you set," the attending physician said, offering consolation. As Suman uttered the words, "Go in peace, my brother," Jeevan's gaze was fixed on Paul. I climbed into the final bed we would share, my heart aching.

I remembered the other beds we had used together. We had shortened our honeymoon to assist with caregiving responsibilities eight years earlier, when we were medical students, and had slept similarly snugly in a twin bed beside my grandfather as he lay dying at home. My affection for Paul grew as I observed him lean in and pay close attention to my grandfather's hushed requests as we woke up every few hours to administer his medication. We never would have thought that Paul's deathbed would be so close to us. We had sobbed in a bed on a different floor of the same hospital twenty-two months prior when we were informed that Paul had been diagnosed with cancer. The day after Cady was born, eight months ago, we were cuddled in my hospital bed, napping together. It was the first deep, restful sleep I'd had since she was born. I recalled falling in love in New Haven twelve years prior, was immediately taken aback by how well our bodies and limbs fit together, and reflected on how, ever since, we had both slept best when entwined. I also thought of our comfortable bed at home, empty. I fervently hoped that he now experienced the same peaceful comfort.

After an hour, Paul's IV was filled with morphine, and the mask and monitors had been turned off. He seemed at ease, and his breathing was shallow but steady. But when I asked if he needed more morphine, he closed his eyes and nodded in agreement. His father's hand was on his head, and his mother sat close. He eventually lost consciousness.

As Paul, now unconscious, drew increasingly halting, infrequent breaths, his eyelids closed, his face unburdened, his family—his parents, brothers, sister-in-law, daughter, and me—sat vigil for over nine hours. He gently put his long fingers in mine. After holding Cady in their arms, Paul's parents put her back in bed to cuddle, nurse, and sleep. Overflowing with affection, the space reflected the numerous weekends and holidays we had all shared over the years. In addition to whispering, "You're a brave Paladin," which is my nickname for Paul, I caressed his hair and softly sang into his ear a favorite jingle we had composed over the previous few months, which had as its main theme, "Thank you for loving me." After our pastor, a close relative and uncle showed up. After the family shared heartwarming stories and inside jokes, we all took turns crying and worriedly examined Paul's and each other's faces, immersed in the pain and sensitivity of these final hours spent together.

As Paul's breaths became quieter, warm evening light started to slant through the room's northwest-facing window. A family friend came to take her home as Cady rubbed her eyes with plump fists as bedtime drew near. With tufts of their matching dark hair equally disheveled, I held her cheek to Paul's. His face was calm and serene, while hers was calm and questioning. His darling baby didn't know this was goodbye. I released Cady after softly singing her bedtime song to her and the two of them.

Paul's breathing became labored and erratic as the room grew darker into night, with a low wall lamp casting a warm glow. His limbs were relaxed, and his body still seemed to be at rest. With his eyes closed and his lips parted, Paul took a deep breath just before nine o'clock and let it out.

———

Because of Paul's rapid decline, When Breath Becomes Air is somewhat incomplete, but that is a necessary part of its truth and the reality Paul had to deal with. Paul wrote nonstop in the final year of his life, driven by a sense of urgency and purpose. While still a neurosurgery chief resident, he began with midnight bursts, tapping away on his laptop as he lay beside me in bed. Later, he spent afternoons in his recliner, wrote paragraphs in the waiting room of his oncologist, answered calls from his editor while receiving chemotherapy, and carried his silver laptop with him everywhere he went. We discovered seamless, silver-lined gloves that enabled him to use a trackpad and keyboard when his chemotherapy-induced finger fissures became painful. His palliative-care appointments focused on strategies for maintaining the mental focus required to write in spite of the punishing fatigue of progressive cancer. He was committed to continuing to write.

This book conveys the sense of urgency that comes with having important things to say in a hurry. As a doctor and a patient, Paul faced death head-on—analyzed it, fought it, and came to terms with it. He wished to assist people in confronting their mortality and understanding death. Nowadays, it is uncommon to die in one's fourth decade, but dying is not. In an email to his best friend Robin, Paul stated, "The thing about lung cancer is that it's not exotic." "It's just imaginable enough and tragic enough." "So that's what it looks like from here...sooner or later I'll be back here in my own shoes," the reader can say after putting themselves in these shoes and taking a few steps. I believe that's what I'm going for. This is what lies ahead on the road, not the sensationalism of dying or the urging to gather rosebuds. He didn't just describe the terrain, of course. He bravely walked through it.

In our death-avoidant society, Paul's choice to keep his eyes open to death is a testament to a strength we don't honor enough. Besides ambition and hard work, his strength was characterized by softness, which is the antithesis of bitterness. His book delves into the crucial area of how to live a meaningful life, a question he grappled with for much of his life. Emerson wrote, "The seer is always a sayer." "Somehow he publishes it with solemn joy; somehow his dream is told." Writing this book gave this brave seer the opportunity to speak up and teach us how to deal with death in a morally upright manner.

Until this book was published, the majority of our family and friends would not have known about the marital issues Paul and I faced near the end of his stay. However, I'm happy Paul wrote about it. It is a component of our reality, an additional redefinition, a part of Paul's and my life's struggle, redemption, and significance. We were able to return to the tender, filling meat of our marriage after his cancer diagnosis was like a nutcracker. Our love was stripped bare, and we clung to one another for both our emotional and physical survival. Each of us made a joke to close friends about how one person's terminal illness is the key to preserving a relationship. On the other hand, we were aware that being genuinely in love—to be open, compassionate, giving, and thankful—is one way to cope with a terminal illness. We stood side by side in a church pew and sang the hymn "The Servant Song" a few months after his diagnosis. The words, "I will share your joy and sorrow / Till we've seen this journey through," rang with meaning as we faced pain and uncertainty together.

Paul's declaration to me right after his diagnosis to get married again after he passed away was a perfect example of how he would put in a lot of effort to ensure my future even while he was ill. He was fervently dedicated to making sure I had the best life possible, including our financial situation, my career, and what motherhood would entail. The most significant doctoring role of my life was to track and manage every symptom and aspect of his medical care, while also supporting his ambitions, listening to his whispered fears as we embraced in the safety of our darkened bedroom, and witnessing, acknowledging, accepting, and comforting him. At the same time, I worked hard to secure his present and make the most of his remaining time. When we held hands during lectures, we were just as bonded as we had been as medical students. Even in warm weather, Paul wore a winter coat and hat, and we now held hands in his coat pocket while taking walks outside following chemotherapy. He was aware that he would never be left alone or endure needless suffering. "Can you breathe okay with my head on your chest like this?" I asked him in bed at home a few weeks before he died. "It's the only way I know how to breathe," was his response. One of the greatest blessings I have ever experienced is that Paul and I were able to contribute to the profound significance of each other's lives.

We both found strength in Paul's family, who helped us get through his illness and helped us welcome our own child into the world. Despite being devastated by their son's illness, his parents continued to be a constant source of solace and stability. They rented a nearby apartment and went there frequently, with Paul's mother preparing Indian dosa with coconut chutney and his father massaging his feet. With Paul's legs propped up to ease his back pain, Suman, Jeevan, and Paul relaxed on our couches while talking about the "syntax" of football plays. While Cady and her cousins, Eve and James, were napping, Jeevan's wife, Emily, and I were laughing close by. Our living room felt like a little, secure village on those afternoons. Later, while I took pictures, Paul would read aloud from works by

Wittgenstein, T. S. Eliot, and Robert Frost while holding Cady in his writing chair in the same room. Such uncomplicated moments were infused with elegance, beauty, and even luck, if luck is a concept at all. However, we were fortunate and thankful for our daughter, our family, our community, our opportunity, and the fact that we had come together at a time when complete acceptance and trust were needed. These past few years have been the most beautiful and profound of my life, although they have also been the most painful and challenging— at times nearly impossible. They have required me to constantly balance life and death, joy and pain, and to reach new heights of thankfulness and love.

Paul faced every stage of his illness with dignity, not with bluster or a misplaced belief that he would "overcome" or "beat" cancer, but with an authenticity that allowed him to mourn the loss of the future he had planned and create a new one. He did so relying on his own strength and the support of his family and community. The day he was diagnosed, he sobbed. A drawing we had on the bathroom mirror that read, "I want to spend all the rest of my days here with you," brought tears to his eyes. On his final day in the operating room, he shed tears. He allowed himself to be consoled, to be open and vulnerable. Paul was fully alive even though he was terminally ill; he remained active, open, and hopeful—not for an unlikely cure, but for days that were full of meaning and purpose—despite his physical collapse.

Paul has a powerful, unique, and somewhat lonesome voice in When Breath Becomes Air. The love, warmth, openness, and radical permission that surrounded him parallel this story. Each of us has a distinct identity in both space and time. Here he is in a doctor-patient relationship, as a patient, and as a doctor. Though there were other selves as well, he wrote in a clear voice, the voice of someone with little time and a relentless drive. Paul's sense of humor—he was wickedly funny—his sweetness and tenderness, and the importance he placed on friendships and family ties are not entirely conveyed in these pages. But when he needed to write something, he wrote it. This is the book he wrote; this was his voice during this time; this was his message during this time. In fact, the Paul who wrote this book—frail but never weak—is the Paul I miss the most, even more than the strong, brilliant Paul with whom I fell in love in the first place. He was a beautiful, focused man in his final year.

Paul was proud of this book because it was the result of his passion for reading (he once claimed that poetry was more consoling to him than the Bible) and his ability to weave a compelling story about coping with death from his own life. "The good news is I've already outlived two Brontës, Keats, and Stephen Crane," Paul wrote in an email to his best friend in May 2013 when he told him he had terminal cancer. I haven't written anything, which is bad news. From one ardent career to another, from husband to father, and, of course, from life to death—the ultimate metamorphosis that awaits us all—his journey was one of change. I am honored to have been his companion from the beginning to the end, including during the writing of this book, which enabled him to live with hope and the delicate alchemy of opportunity and agency about which he writes so beautifully.

—

With a view of the Pacific Ocean and a coastline full of memories—brisk hikes, seafood feasts, and birthday cocktails—Paul was laid to rest in a willow casket at the edge of a field in the Santa Cruz Mountains. On a warm January weekend two months prior, we had dipped Cady's plump feet in the salty water at a beach below. He left it up to us to decide what should happen to his body after he passed away because he was not attached to it. I think we made a wise decision. Paul's grave faces the ocean to the west, across five miles of verdant hilltops. The hills surrounding him are covered with yellow euphorbia, conifers and wild grass. You can hear the wind, birds chirping, and chipmunks scuffling as you sit down. His grave site feels suitably rugged and honorable, a place he deserves to be—a place we all deserve to be—and he arrived here on his own terms. "We shall rise insensibly, and reach the tops of the everlasting hills, where the winds are cool and the sight is glorious," is a line from a blessing that my grandfather enjoyed that comes to mind.

However, it's not always easy to be here. The weather is erratic. I have visited Paul in the midst of scorching sun, hazy fog, and freezing, stinging rain because he is buried on the windward side of the mountains. There is beauty in all of it, and I believe this is good and right. It can be both peaceful and uncomfortable, communal and lonely—like death, like grief.

I frequently go to his grave with a tiny bottle of Madeira wine, which was the destination of our honeymoon. I pour some on the grass for Paul every time. When Paul's brothers and parents are around, I rub the grass like Paul's hair while we converse. Before she naps, Cady goes to his grave, where she lies on a blanket, watches the clouds fly by, and snatches at the flowers we've placed. When our siblings and I got together with twenty of Paul's closest and oldest friends the night before his memorial service, I momentarily questioned whether we would ruin the grass by spilling so much whiskey.

I frequently go back to the grave after leaving flowers, such as carnations, tulips, and lilies, to discover that the deer have eaten the heads. Paul would have approved this use for flowers, which is as good as any other. Worms swiftly turn the earth over, and the natural processes continue their march, reminding me of what Paul witnessed and what I now deeply believe: the inevitability of life and death and the capacity to cope and find purpose in spite of this. Paul was no tragedy, but what happened to him was.

After Paul's death, I thought I would only feel heartbroken and empty. I had no idea that you could love someone the same way after he passed away, that I would still feel such love and thankfulness in addition to the awful grief, which is so heavy that sometimes I shiver and groan under its weight. Even though I miss Paul terribly almost all the time, I feel like I'm still contributing to the life we built together. According to C. S. Lewis, "bereavement is one of its regular phases—

like the honeymoon—rather than the truncation of married love." Our goal is to remain faithful and healthy during that time in our marriage. Taking care of our daughter, fostering family ties, publishing this book, seeking fulfilling employment, going to Paul's grave, mourning and paying tribute to him, and persevering—my love endures—lives on—in a manner I never would have imagined.

I realized that Paul would have made significant contributions as a neurosurgeon and neuroscientist if he had survived when I visited the hospital where he lived and passed away as a patient and a doctor. The work that initially drew him to neurosurgery would have allowed him to assist innumerable patients and their families during some of the most trying times in their lives. He was a good man and a serious thinker, and he would have remained so. Rather, this book is a fresh approach to helping others that only he could provide. This does not lessen the pain of his passing or our loss. But the striving had meaning for him. He stated, "You can believe in an asymptote toward which you are ceaselessly striving, but you can never reach perfection," on page 115 of this book. It was hard, painful labor, but he never gave up. This is how he lived the life that was given to him. As it is, When Breath Becomes Air it is whole.

"When someone dies, people tend to say great things about him," I wrote in my journal, two days after Paul's passing, and addressed it to Cady. Please know that everything that people are saying about your dad right now is accurate. He was truly courageous and talented. The lyrics of the hymn from The Pilgrim's Progress, "Who would true valour see, / Let him come hither.../ Then fancies fly away, / He'll fear not what men say, / He'll labor night and day / To be a pilgrim," frequently come to mind when I think about his purpose. Paul's choice to face death head-on demonstrated not only who he was in his last hours but also who he had always been. Paul pondered death and whether he could face it honorably for much of his life. Ultimately, the response was affirmative.

I was a witness and his wife.

Printed in Dunstable, United Kingdom